MAKING
MONEY
MATTER

MAKING MONEY MATTER

IMPACT INVESTING TO CHANGE THE WORLD!

by

G. Benjamin Bingham, CFP

PROSPECTA PRESS

WESTPORT, CONNECTICUT 2015

Published by
Prospecta Press
An imprint of Easton Studio Press
P.O. Box 3131
Westport, CT 06880
(203) 571-0781

www.prospectapress.com

10 9 8 7 6 5 4 3 2 1

Book and cover design by Barbara Aronica-Buck (www.bookdesigner.com)
Cover art by Andrey Armyagov, Shutterstock
Author photo by Kent Corley Photography (www.kentcorley.com)

Hardcover ISBN: 978-1-63226-023-9
eBook ISBN: 978-1-63226-024-6

First edition

Manufactured in the United States of America
First printing, April 2015

DEDICATION

The State Department honored my father, Hiram Bingham IV, posthumously with the 2002 American Foreign Service Award for Constructive Dissent for the actions he took to free Jewish families from Vichy France in 1941. Along with his journals, he had hidden letters from Mark Chagall and other well-known artists and writers from this time behind our colonial-era fireplace, to be discovered after he died. *I dedicate this book to his courageous dissent.*

ACKNOWLEDGMENTS

Thanks to all who have given me new perspectives and supported me in developing my own. To my wife, Jenny, who is my best coach and supporter and fills my life with color and nourishment, both earthly and otherwise.

To my core team in our advisory and fund management work: Marnita Butler, Jessy Joyce Nadar, and Angelina Bellochio, for your courage and tenacity in the face of all challenges and your professional standards and patience despite my sometimes slow learning curve. This has been a long journey.

To our loyal clients, who have stayed with us through thick and thin. To all my friends and advisors, including consultants and generous readers of this book in its earlier forms—you are too numerous to all be mentioned. You know who you are. Thank you. And special thanks to Sally Goerner who helped me form my thoughts and added her own essay on fractals; to Susan Axelrod, my original copyeditor, who dared question financial language when it was not her own; and to Bill Endicott, who challenged me to make it a masterpiece. Special thanks also to Lisa Renstrom, who encouraged me to speak my truth without apology, and to my old friend David Wilk for believing in me and this book.

To my children who have grown into adults, Gareth, Candor, Simon, Elias, and Nathan—you have been my teachers as I see myself mirrored in each of you . . . you are moving humanity on a touch more than I will. Thus we evolve. And last, to my four granddaughters, Jebetu, Maya Rose, Tiger Lily, and Tallulah— thank you for brightening my life and giving me hope.

TABLE OF CONTENTS

FOREWORD

By Cathy Clark, Jed Emerson, and Ben Thornley

From its origins in socially responsible investing, community finance, microfinance, and international development, impact investing has emerged as a distinct practice. This has warranted the creation of new field-level infrastructure, including the Global Impact Investing Network and Impact Investing Policy Collaborative.[1,2] It has also motivated volumes of excellent research, adding tremendous depth to the conversation among practitioners.[3]

The three of us, together with colleagues at Pacific Community Ventures and CASE at Duke, have spent the last three years shifting the discussion from the "why" of impact investing to the "how," by examining the practices and performance of twelve outstanding funds in detail, culled from an initial list of 350.[4] Our recently released book, *The Impact Investor: Lessons in Leadership and Strategy for Collaborative Capitalism* (John Wiley & Sons), also connects the experiences of the twelve funds to the bigger picture of a more outcomes-oriented, transparent, and responsive form of business and finance writ large.

What the twelve funds demonstrate is that, while inherently diverse in its application, impact investing is in fact a cohesive discipline. With decades of practice to draw upon, there is no need to speculate on what impact investing might be or debate whether it is possible for investors to receive financial returns along with social and/or environmental impacts. This level of doubt was warranted in the 1.0 era, but the twelve funds we studied prove the opposite.

The bottom line is this: a first generation of private impact investing funds has delivered on the promise of concurrently delivering financial returns and explicit social outcomes.

Developed and emerging market equity and hybrid funds, all with some participation of commercial investors aiming for market-rate performance, have generated financial returns of 3–22 percent. Social debt funds—with primarily individual, philanthropic or policy-driven bank investors—have returned 0–3 percent, matching their targets and never losing a dime.

We can now enter a "2.0 generation" of impact investing with confidence, knowing what practices undergird success and building on these lessons to bring the field to scale.

Outstanding impact investing funds undertake many practices common to all asset managers; they carefully nurture their brand, leverage all of the relationships at their disposal, are often headed or backed by singularly reputable or experienced individuals and institutions, demonstrate exceptional financial discipline, are models of operational excellence, and work relentlessly to support the growth of their investees. However, there are particular characteristics that set impact investing funds apart:

First: Though not a necessity, many funds actively maintain relationships with government, either seeking direct investment from public entities or leveraging other policy incentives. And the relationship is not one-sided. The funds also use their experience in the field to influence the creation of more enabling and supportive public policy environments.

Second: Many funds benefit from what we call Catalytic Capital: when one set of investments triggers additional capital that may not have otherwise been available to a fund, enterprise, sector, or geography, thereby generating exponential social or environmental value. We know that investors providing capital for strategic in addition to financial reasons have been critical to the development of impact investing; however, we did not expect Catalytic Capital to have been so prevalent.

Catalytic Capital in the form of grants, guarantees, or concessionary or cornerstone investments may have the potential to negatively distort markets, particularly at the investee level. However at the fund level, our studies show Catalytic Capital has been nothing short of transformative, unlocking billions of dollars of non-catalytic investments.

Third: Many impact fund founders and leaders have a high degree of cross-cultural, cross-sector, and multilingual capacities. Those responsible for making investments must execute with unshakable financial discipline, but successful fund leadership is about more than simply effective money management. Cross-sector experience can be observed in multiple essential areas: finance/business, policy, and impact/philanthropy.

Multilingual Leadership takes this notion a step further and indicates the institutionalization of a fund's ability to move seamlessly among diverse stakeholders and audiences.

Finally, the leading impact funds have shown that they are able to move beyond the conventional wisdom of the 1.0 era which assumed that any approach to impact investing had to choose between either a financial-first or impact-first lens. In fact we have seen that this is rarely the case. In reality, funds put financial and social objectives on an equal footing by establishing a clearly embedded strategy and structure for achieving mission *prior* to investment, enabling a predominantly financial focus *throughout* the life of the investment.

Knowing early and explicitly that impact is in a fund's DNA, all parties (investors, investees, and the fund itself) are able to move forward with the investment disciplines akin to any other financial transaction, confident that mission drift is unlikely. Towards the end of the investment, the focus of funds returns to the impact achieved according to a stated mission. "Mission First and Last" demonstrates that, in practice, every fund combines *explicit impact intention* with *operational accountability to impact,* and suggests that it is time to retire our dichotomous financial-first or impact-first thinking.

Making Money Matter: Impact Investing to Change the World is an important contribution to the body of knowledge and thought leadership essential for the further growth of Impact Investing. Ben Bingham is a veteran impact investor who has been in the trenches and can guide us in a unique and imaginative way to an understanding of money's potential as a tool for doing well by doing good.

INTRODUCTION

May 2014 marked the end of the world as I knew it. Along with a number of economists and thought leaders, I traveled to St. Augustine, Florida, for a gathering called *Finding Ethical Alpha.* Hazel Henderson, the *grande dame* of new economic thinking, had brought us there. After predicting much of what has unfolded since the 1970s, now Hazel beams out rays of hopeful data from her website (www.ethicalmarkets.com), where she tracks the new Green Economy— global spending is already in the trillions and accelerating.

But the news in the room that day was not all warm and fuzzy. We realized that we were witnessing a time of global change that could prematurely end what Hazel calls the "Age of the Anthropocene." Humankind may become as extinct as the dinosaurs.

It seems there are two ways out of this dilemma: one following the simple wisdom of nature and Hazel's "exponential growth in consciousness," and the other employing a plethora of technological solutions. This is a time of global reckoning. The future is not known, but is more than ever in our own hands. The question is whether we will support the proliferation of ready solutions, or continue to invest in the problems.

If we embrace the energy of the sun, the wind, and the rising tides (together able to provide twenty-four times the energy we currently consume), will we do it in a way that remembers the soul? Will the future of humanity be wedded with the living and dying rhythms of nature? Or will we be mechanized and digitized to the point that human error becomes redundant—and cyber-biotic beings replace our gentle genus?

Katherine Collins, the former head of research at Fidelity and author of *The Nature of Investing*, elegantly demonstrated that there is too much uncertainty about the future to depend on data from the past. We would better order our investments with policies, procedures, and processes that are in harmony with nature—in the "how" and the "why" of our investing. It is abundantly clear that our relationships define the quality of our life, especially our relationship with nature and "spirit," however we choose to define it. Because we have lost touch with nature, we find ourselves in the current predicament: destroying our own home planet.

Dennis Bushnell, Chief Scientist at NASA Langley Research Center, brought our attention to the chilling fact that natural disasters are likely to wipe us out unless we act now. In fact it may already be too late. In the 1980s, he predicted that, given the rate of global warming, all Arctic ice would melt by 2100. So far, his theories have been proven correct. Moreover, the global buildup of methane is increasing the likelihood that tsunamis will form. But Bushnell claims we already have the means to solve most of our problems. For example:

1. Halophytes, plants that are prolific when irrigated with sea-water, could green the Sahara and provide sufficient biomass to replace all fossil fuels, feed the hungry, and provide fresh water for human use.[5]

2. Hydrogen power is ready to go, with the first large-scale utility already built in South Korea.[6]

3. The biofuel company Joule Unlimited has created a synthetic gasoline alternative, produced cheaply by exposing CO_2 in brackish water to sunlight.[7]

4. LENR (Low Energy Nuclear Reaction) holds extraordinary promise, but is still risky and controversial. (Recently an explosion in a NASA lab melted the glass in the windows.)[8]

We have the means to power the world harmlessly, yet 85 percent of our current energy use is needlessly harmful to the planet, which speeds up the rate of global "weirding." Will we wake up in time? Will we invest to survive, or better, for future generations to thrive? You will decide with your money! How it is spent, loaned, borrowed, gifted, or invested will determine the planet's future. Welcome to the new economics: prosperity will only be realized if we take care of ourselves and the planet.

So what are we going to do about it? We must form a global community, and move trillions of dollars, to accelerate solutions to the urgent problems of our time. This is not a pipe dream, but rather a necessity and a smart strategy for investors. After fourteen years of advising insightful investors, I have dwelled inside the "belly of the beast," and having seen the innards of our current financial world, I am awake to the need for change.

Following a misguided sense of fiduciary duty, the people and institutions with the most resources are investing in a world that could self-destruct. Their advisors encourage them to stick with the profitable status quo. Meanwhile, like "prudent lemmings" lining up on the edge of a fiscal cliff, investors are quite skeptical of anything but "plain vanilla" investing. One goal of this book is to urge traditional investors to wake up from this complacency by providing them with a whole financial ecosystem of sophisticated investment strategies.

Because of my lifelong love of Benjamin Franklin's wit and wisdom, I have included reflections on the thirteen virtues he used to guide his own actions. Virtue in the context of investment might have been considered an anomaly on Wall Street in the past, but this is changing rapidly.

This book traces my own journey out of financial innocence

and towards an investment model that supports reasonable returns, long-term economic health, and a healthy future for our planet. There are many books on money and investing, but very few build a bridge from philosophical values to practical understanding and advice. If you allow your thinking to change, you will find new ways to spend, lend, invest, and gift your financial resources.

"Socially Responsible Investing" (SRI) has grown dramatically in recent years. There are many public options to invest in mutual funds that screen out negatives, invest proactively, or promote activist strategies to improve corporate governance and environmental and social standards. "Impact Investing," or purely proactive problem-solving investment, is taking hold in the private sector, particularly in massive infrastructure projects and environmental cleanup. *Making Money Matter* provides an inclusive overview, giving practical advice while demonstrating how to move trillions of investor dollars towards solving the world's many dire problems.

• • •

Socially conscious investing is both personal and practical in a profound way. As investors open themselves up to new possibilities and relationships with money, they become empowered to take action. This burgeoning movement links modern financial intelligence with core ethical and environmental tenets to form a powerful matrix for wise investing.

The values presented are not sectarian; they are practical, pragmatic, and universally human. There is room for many interpretations once money is seen primarily as a tool for taking care of our unique needs. The new mission of money is to meet universal needs that do not infringe upon society at large, but instead support our shared planet. It is in everyone's interest to shift in this direction. To end the abuses of Wall Street, big banks, and our current financial system, we must change economic thinking to include ourselves ("as if people mattered" as E. F. Schumacher put it), whether we are average investors, businessmen, progressives, libertarians, or fiscal conservatives.

If you have read George Clason's classic inspirational book, *The Richest Man in Babylon,* you already know the key idea (and I am divulging the secret here) is to "pay yourself first"—that is, set aside 10 percent (more if you are older) of whatever you earn and invest it in the future. Clason does not, however, indicate *how* to invest it. The same is true for the so-called "divestment movement"; it is one thing not to invest in bad stuff, but who will guide you once you divest?

If you are socially conscious, you might decide against the global casino called "the market." You might instead foster one great business idea and put your heart and soul and extra money into it. But once hard times hit, you would have to sheepishly return to your advisor and let the "expert" take charge.

• • •

You might decide to stick with fairly safe low-interest loans from a group such as the Reinvestment Fund or RSF Social Finance and enjoy a slow and steady pace of growth compared to a roller-coaster investment ride.[9,10] None of these decisions are inherently right or wrong. You must discover what makes sense for you.

Everyone is different, but everyone uses money, and the way we think about money has more impact than all the impact investments put together. Fundamental economic thinking needs to change. Just as consumers drove supermarkets to buy local and organic food, investors will drive the new money paradigm.

It's currently very difficult to shop for good companies or social enterprises to invest in. This experience must:

1. Become more user friendly,

2. Offer a broad selection of investments to choose from,

3. Include professional infrastructure and consultant support that is institutionally trustworthy.

Financially, the process of finding good investments will not fundamentally change. Products and services that are unique and designed for the long term will be the winners. The most conscious and conscientious investors, however, will realize that durable enterprises must be sustainable from a social and environmental perspective. For example, Al Gore's environmentally aware investment firm, Generation, prefers to define its investments not as socially responsible or sustainable, but simply as "long term."[11] The premise of Generation is that companies that ignore potential environmental disasters are too short-term oriented and should be avoided, whereas problem solvers will last. This common-sense way of thinking is becoming more standard fare.

For the new money paradigm to work, all hands are needed on deck. "Standard fare" will not be enough. Profitable technological innovations and new business models will drive the new economy, while improved physical and technological infrastructure will lift up local and global communities. Awareness and empathy for workers and for the planet as a whole will be expressed in the price of goods and services. We can sidestep many long-term problems if we:

1. Learn to reduce, reuse, and recycle more, avoiding extraction as much as possible;

2. Relearn time-tested natural ways of living and avoid questionable synthetic products; and

3. Learn to respect each other and our world, avoiding the degradation of nature and society as best we can. (See the Natural Step in Chapter 9.)

• • •

Why am I qualified to write this book? I have been a social entrepreneur for decades, helping to develop innovative solutions for key social and environmental problems. I was educated at Groton School, Yale, and Emerson College in England, where I first learned some of the new thinking about money as described by Rudolf Steiner (*Rethinking Economics*) and E. F. Schumacher (*Small Is Beautiful: Economics as if People Mattered*).[12,13] In 1978, after a few years as a biodynamic farmer, I co-founded a nonprofit enterprise, a sustainable agricultural community for learning-disabled young people. In the 1990s, I helped start two for-profit socially responsible technology companies in biological health and Internet workflow. I worked with philanthropically minded investors for all these ventures, which are all continuing today. I have the advantage of a fresh perspective not entrenched in tired financial models from the last century.

In the early 2000s, I became a financial advisor and certified wealth manager, first at Legg Mason and later as a Certified Financial Planner (CFP) at Smith Barney. Desiring independence from the extraordinary limitations of big banks, I left to develop new ways of investing: to make money for clients and make an environmental and social impact. In the last seven years, I have continuously worked on developing model financial ecosystems for my clients.

In April of 2012, we launched the first five impact funds, which combine years of research and development all focused on above-market returns and maximized benefits for all stakeholders. These funds strive to be productive both in their financial performance and in terms of affirming and enhancing life.

Meanwhile, during these years the rich were getting richer and the poor poorer, while the new middle class kept demanding more stuff. Darwin's theories are sometimes wrongly used to argue that materialistic competition is an evolutionary necessity. However, the current dysfunctional world economy is the ultimate and unsustainable outcome of this amoral competitive approach to life. The horrific polarization of rich and poor sparked the Occupy Wall Street movement, which bemoans the fact that 1 percent of the population, in this country and globally, control 99 percent of the resources. Trustees of vast resources are frozen by a false concept of fiduciary duty, thinking, as has been argued in court, that this term refers only to making as much money as possible, no matter what.

Some pension funds have begun to question this nonsense, but the movement needs to be much broader to push prices of dangerous and irresponsible stocks in a downward direction. Adam Kanzer, the Managing Director and General Counsel of Domini Social Investments, argues that this may not happen until the indices that serve as "benchmarks" for public funds remove harmful companies from their lists. He strongly rebuts the argument that funds have a "fiduciary duty to maximize profits" by citing the "prudent man standard," which directs trustees to "observe how men of prudence, discretion and intelligence manage their own affairs." Kanzer argues that "It is self-evident that a prudent person would not use her own money to harm her children. It is both callous and misguided to suggest that fiduciaries are compelled to do so."[14]

A simple framework for prudent investing is to prioritize deals that are good deals for everyone, including the environment. This is not so easy in practice. The key question, which must be faced over and over again to maintain balance and avoid extremes, is simply this: What is most important, with everyone in mind?

The environment is something we all share. As the Gulf Stream cools, winters will grow longer in Ireland and Northern

Europe. We are now at 400 parts per million of carbon in the atmosphere, well beyond the neutral point of 350 ppm. We must do something drastic, and soon.

It may be too late to stem the tide of environmental disaster, material greed, and military terror, yet everyone will benefit if we do so. The intervention of the Occupy movement has reawakened in millions their natural capacity for ethics, their common sense for what is right, and their innate capacity for empathy and altruism. Now is the time to be urgently optimistic.

Behind all the many *consciousness* movements currently bubbling up around the world, there is a more or less conscious tendency to think holistically—constructing beliefs and action plans based on the underlying reality that all things are connected. We are all related. Some would include both the spiritual and the physical in this oneness. It is the thinking behind money that unites meaning with matter.

The Occupy movement will continue to evolve as long as individuals are willing to take responsibility for themselves and for their world. The hope for the future is in the free individual who prioritizes "doing the good" for others. Not all will devote themselves to things that truly matter. But as more do so, we shall attain a culture of "ethical individualism," the standard Rudolf Steiner set for a healthy future. In Chapter 12 I will delve into Steiner's approach to money and his vision of the ideal restructuring of society.

If you have not heard of Rudolf Steiner, you are not alone. Many well-known individuals and organizations have embraced his innovative and practical insights from the early twentieth century, without much acknowledgement. Steiner approached life not as a specialist, but as a creative generalist with spiritual vision. In his day, he gave lectures all over Europe and Great Britain to audiences of thousands; his advice was always given in response to a request. Although some of his ideas may seem strange and need time to percolate, they have proven themselves valid in the realms of childhood education, biodynamic agriculture, and social finance.

• • •

Steiner's crucial insight was that a healthy society will come about only to the degree that ethical individuals take responsibility. He was guided by the altruistic vision of a tripartite society with *Liberty* as the leading theme for all culture, *Equality* for all governments, and *Brotherhood* standing behind all commercial transactions. In a sense, responsibility is never "given"; it is "taken," and individuals with strong consciences will *take* the lead.

An economics course Steiner gave in 1922 was recently republished as *Rethinking Economics*. In the Foreword, the popular MIT professor Otto Scharmer presents a ten-point guide to ideas in the course that he considers to be especially pertinent today. (I elaborate on this list in Chapter 11.) In his eighth point, Scharmer writes that a truly healthy economy requires "awareness based on self-regulation of the economic process." One might assume that "awareness-based self-regulation" will never happen, that people will just continue being "only human," motivated primarily by greed and fear, especially around money. Greed and fear are often justified by love for family; for example, we want to protect our own and provide everything they need or desire. But why not be *greedy* for a world we could all enjoy and love? Why not *fear* destructive and polluting corporations that threaten our community and our world?

It makes common sense to invest in what you love and understand. Businesses generally do well when consumers love their products or services. Companies built to take care of needs are generally built to last and prosper for investors. According to portfolio manager Paul Herman, "Today, one out of eight investment dollars seeks 'human impact' as well as profit," while Goldman Sachs has found that publicly listed companies that look for both human impact and profit outperform others.[15]

In the end, Occupy is about the 100 percent. It's about each one of us consciously taking hold, taking responsibility, and joining the great journey of evolution in our own unique way, for the common good. To make money regardless of harm done is unconscionable *and* a mistake. We are partners in the world of finance— what we do with our money ripples throughout the world and comes back to haunt us or heal us. Money is a tool for positive change. What the world now needs are key concepts for a healthy new money paradigm.

Every person's financial history is unique. I choose to share my story here because this particular journey has strengthened me and taught me what is most important.

PART I:

MONEY
LESSONS
LEARNED

CHAPTER 1:

YOUTHFUL IDEALISM (1970–1985)

*"It's better to be absolutely ridiculous
than absolutely boring."* —*Marilyn Monroe*

At the age of twenty-three, I spent $10,000 on a new roof for a crumbling barn that I hardly used and a deep well that I never hooked up. This was one third of my inheritance.

Two years earlier, I had inherited $30,000 from my grandfather and decided to take a leave of absence from Yale after my sophomore year. The Black Panther Revolution was in full force, and a few friends were even talking about blowing up the law school to make a statement, but it made no sense to me to fight a violent system with violence. Due to my high lottery number, I could avoid the violence in Vietnam as well if I left college for a year. I had completed the prerequisites for a major in Fine Arts and Philosophy and already soaked in the best lecturers' survey courses. Without any signature concepts to develop in art form, I wanted more life experience and needed time to think. As it turned out, I never returned.

At my father's encouragement, I enrolled in Emerson College in East Sussex, England, and stayed for the next two years paying my way to study biodynamic agriculture and learning to work with my hands. This training in sustainable agriculture became the basis for most of my work, right down to how I think of financial portfolios as ecosystems. As I prepared to return to my family's farm in Connecticut, the college bookkeeper gave me guidance on how to think about financial bookkeeping, which grew into a study of Steiner's Threefold Social Order.

Other students joined in, and this seminar became part of the curriculum for the next forty years. I was inspired and am forever grateful for this impromptu study that I continue to this day.

I was privileged enough to be born into an old New England family with plenty of land and two dairies managed in the valley. Upon returning home after a tour of biodynamic farms in Europe, I began milking, feeding, harvesting corn, and cleaning out the barn at my uncle's farm. I did this alone for a herd of one hundred cows for $500/month (my first salary). Meanwhile, I rented a small farm for $250/month, building my own herd of black jerseys with a mix of other farm animals. The next year, my wife Jenny joined me, and we had dreams of converting a family barn into a restaurant surrounded by fields of vegetables.

My siblings are now grateful that I invested one third of my inheritance to save the barn and put in a well: forty years later, the barn is now surrounded with someone else's biodynamic veggies in a Community Supported Agriculture (CSA) venture that feeds 200 families. I am glad the money was spent. In retrospect, it taught me to think about long-term consequences and always consider each outlay of capital in relation to short-term affordability *and* long-term intentions.

After my uncle decided to close the dairy and sell the cows, Jenny and I continued to board horses where we were renting. Our annual income from this was only $3,000, and we grew almost everything we ate and seldom went out. We were slowly losing money and gave no thought to replacing the capital spent on the barn and well. But we slept soundly after each day's hard work.

As friends started to join us, we imagined more possibilities— a Waldorf school, worker housing, a community—but my larger family was resistant, and we had no idea how to finance these dreams. Jenny and I decided to join an "intentional community," one with some proven roots, to learn how to make things work. We chose Camphill, an international association of intentional communities with individuals who require special care. The particular community, near Copake, NY, had an experienced farmer looking for an apprentice.

Still in our twenties, we found ourselves responsible for our four children (including twins), all under four years old, while taking care of eight severely handicapped adults in our home. Early before breakfast, I left to milk cows, then spent most of my day co-managing the farm crew and growing three acres of vegetables with workhorses.

After three years, we moved on to co-found a similar intentional community, Triform Camphill, and before we knew it, ten years had passed. Fortunately, social security checks are based on three consecutive best-income years; otherwise, because we were technically volunteers, the ten zero-income years would have significantly dragged down my expected social security check.

During this time I did not invest any of my remaining inheritance! In the late 1970s, certificates of deposit (CDs) went into the high teens. If I had immediately invested all $30,000 in CDs in those years, bonds in the 1980s, or equities in the 1990s, the money might have grown to over a million dollars today. Instead of growing nicely, the inheritance was kept conveniently in a zero-interest checking account, which we drew down gradually for clothes, vacations, and other personal items we were too proud to ask for from the community.

Although the second third of my inheritance was soon depleted, we didn't care at that time. We had no interest in growing our fortune because we expected to stay in this encompassing community for life, and secondly, we had not yet learned that the source of all evil is the *love of money*, not money itself. I know now that setting aside money for the future and saving up for future dreams is a beautiful thing, especially if the investments are working all the time for the good of the planet.

The Camphill organization rallied around a dream to employ workers with disabilities to build high-end Swiss beds. I became the Director of Planning and Development and took a course from the Grantsmanship Center in NYC to learn how to write successful grant proposals. It worked. We had already acquired a small farm for the project, and with grants and a line of credit we were able to convert the barn into a small production facility for the Swiss beds with secondhand equipment paid for by the state of NY. We placed a full-page ad in the *New York Times* (for $40,000), paid for by the Public Welfare Foundation, an organization that loved our entrepreneurial model. The photo, of a woman's naked back lying perfectly aligned on one of our beds, attracted the attention of retailers, and we were soon in business. We assembled $30,000 worth of beds per month with two very moderately handicapped adults working alongside a master craftsman.

Years went by. After I had raised almost a million dollars, I was feeling awkward about the relatively small number of special-needs adults who were able to participate in the venture. But, in fact, the business was not sufficiently profitable because of the cost of imported parts. We would need to scale up to one hundred beds a day and make all the parts ourselves to become viable as a business. To raise that kind of capital, we would have needed equity investors in a for-profit business.

In 1982, I did not fully grasp the beauty and potential of a hybrid company that could combine for-profit businesses with charitable goals. Nowadays, social capital is being "invested" in nonprofits with for-profit business models and vice versa. But back then, the nonprofit board rejected my idea to convert the business to a for-profit model that would regularly donate money to the community. At that time, as far as we knew, it was impossible to create a hybrid model where the line between for-profit and non-profit could be drawn pragmatically.

Instead, the factory barn became a cabinetry shop for building our own residences and other structures for the community. I started working the farm with a pitchfork, a truck I bought with my own money, and a scythe. As a community, we began to build an agricultural enterprise with young people who needed a place to grow and learn. Over the years, an alternative campus for young people developed with agriculture, crafts, baking, and forestry as the work focus. We grew from milking a few cows in a pole barn lashed together from trees, like a makeshift Buddhist temple, to operating a whole farm program out of a proper barn. Today the properties have expanded to 400 acres, with many folks coming to work each day or residing full time.

After getting a grant to build the farmhouse for my extended family of children, a coworker, and residents, I loaned the last $10,000 of my inheritance to complete our house, which I thought Jenny and I would live in forever. But I eventually released the community from its pledge to pay us back. Two years later, Jenny and I decided it was time for others to take our place, and we departed with our five children, an old car, and no money to our name. Looking back, I see that forgiving the loan was taking the easy route out, and that it takes guts to make clear contracts and stick to them.

The impulse to create a utopia has never left me; perhaps we all long for the perfect community, though with very different visions of what that might mean. The experience I had in the 1970s and 1980s was deeply textured, a melding of peasant farming and sophisticated production. I worked with skilled and unskilled workers, wealthy donors and customers, volunteers without assets, and special-needs individuals who were at ease with all classes and varieties of humanity. Despite all the goodwill that drives such a community, when the money grew short, tensions bubbled beneath the surface. It seems to be true even among the most altruistic people in the world: a pie is hard to share when it's just not big enough. This knowledge motivates me today to help move money to where it is needed most.

Money needs to keep moving, and, like white corpuscles in

Benjamin Franklin's Virtues: Humility

"Imitate Jesus and Socrates."

Humility plays a key role in the healthy circulation of money. Investment begins with the attitude of the investor. Similarly, the business leaders or entrepreneurs we invest in have to manage this quality, which is usually associated with selflessness or altruism.

According to *Egonomics,* published in 2007 by Marcum and Smith, most businesspeople consider ego the "most expensive liability" in any company.[16] Ego is often associated with self-absorbed personalities that blindly trample over others, losing key employees and contracts in the process. This interpretation is simplistic. The study concluded that great leaders are able to choose between dualities, that balanced leadership is characterized by the flexibility to choose when to be assertive and when to be receptive, direct or diplomatic, intense or easygoing. The ego that chooses dynamically is not dominated by self-interest but, like the good heart, is able to respond with humility as needs arise.

The healthy circulation of money takes into account inherent dualities between investing and philanthropy, lending and simple exchange. There are times to buy and times to sell, to borrow or to lend, to invest or seek investors. The new money paradigm requires the capacity to choose wisely, so that both sides of each transaction benefit mutually and all stakeholders indirectly affected are likewise enriched by the interchange. Driving this paradigm shift is a particular kind of humility driven by constructive discontent—the kind that created today's wave of social capitalism.

CHAPTER 2

MAKING A LIVING (1985–1992)

*"The price of our vitality is the
sum of all our fears." —David Whyte*

When Jenny and I left Triform and briefly visited her family
and friends in South Africa, we suddenly realized how few people
in our generation were raising five children while traipsing around
the world. We certainly had not appreciated our good fortune to
have all our children enrolled in a private Waldorf school, nurtured
with biodynamic produce in a beautiful setting. Although my
social security statement shows ten years of zero income, we had
lived well while working hard. Income is only part of the equation
regarding wealth; quality of life makes up most of it.

"Working for a living" is a common phrase that seems backwards to me. In a chapter of *Small Is Beautiful* called "Buddhist
Economics," Schumacher pointed out that it would be a happier
world if, like the ideal Buddhists, we "lived to work." In other
words, we might choose to work if we had a free choice instead of
being forced to work for a living. To add insult to this form of
enslavement, people are not paid enough to live, and even a
so-called "living wage" just barely covers costs. Why are we so
mean-spirited about this? I felt privileged to work without wages
for ten years; I never worked harder and certainly never regretted
the experience, though our nest egg wasn't growing.

After returning to the United States, we eventually landed in
the woods of New Hampshire. Our lack of cash and resultant frugality gave birth to many creative entrepreneurial solutions. We

could easily have drifted into low self-esteem and lowered expectations, even perhaps the infectious effects of a poverty mentality. Instead we enjoyed living in a dream shack over a crystal-clear stream, where our cat's water bowl sometimes froze indoors and our four older children slept in bunk beds, squeezed into a tiny room. In exchange for free rent, I put in another layer of recycled storm windows, rebuilt the rotten deck, and crawled under the shack to install insulation, my head encased in mosquito netting, all in my free time.

Meanwhile my vocational experiences expanded as I took a job as a carpenter to help finish building a new local Waldorf School that we wanted our children to attend. The hourly rate, along with Jenny's social work and waitressing, would not cover tuition for five children, so I became the manual arts teacher and maintenance man at the school for the next two years. Eventually, though, I needed to earn more money to move into a larger home and pay all the bills.

With no degree, yet with plenty of motivation and fundraising skills, sales seemed an obvious choice. I took the W. Clement Stone sales training program, daring to go door-to-door with no salary, just the power of my conviction. I devoured the training and, using debt as a motivator, purchased two houses on one property with the help of a relative. I went crazy selling door-to-door twelve hours a day to earn promotional awards and fatter assignments. After attaining the "Grand Diamond Award" for selling at breakneck speed, I was introduced to W. Clement Stone himself (the grand wizard of Aon Corporation), hired a sales team, and was assigned my own district. All of this occurred before I realized that my soul had become vacuous, with no space for anything internal beyond motivating mantras like "Do It Now!" and "Conceive, Believe, Achieve!"

Debt, while touted as the American way, is certainly not a healthy motivator. Nevertheless, the experience of facing one rejection after another made me stronger. And real estate does not always increase in value—it rises and falls in cycles: by the time we decided to leave chilly New Hampshire for North Carolina, our property had peaked 30 percent above the cost price, then dropped 15 percent below after computer giants Wang and Digital lost favor and thousands of local employees were laid off. We abandoned our property to the same kind relative, who managed to avoid losing money after expending a great deal of time and energy.

Meanwhile, I had chosen not to enroll in the matching retirement program at Aon because it only vested in six years—certainly I would not be working as a career salesman that long! As it turned out, I continued to work part-time for the firm while temporarily teaching at a new Waldorf School in North Carolina. If I had enrolled in the program, then by the time I finally cut the cord, I would have nicely replaced my original inheritance! Instead I got zilch.

The matching retirement plans that were established in the 1960s produced more millionaires than you might imagine. Those days are mostly over, however, as corporations cut costs by switching from defined benefits to defined contributions, and as retirement plans fail to grow. Since the turn of the new millennium, the most popular investment index, the S&P 500, grew from January 2000 to January 2014 by 27.8 percent, while the average cost of living increased by over 37.7 percent.[17,18] That means that after inflation, the S&P returned a loss of –7.753 percent in terms of buying power. The numbers change constantly and the future is uncertain, but with innovation and positive commitment, values tend to rebound. We'll see.

INFLATION

To give you a better idea of how fluid the value of dollars can be, inflation rates in the last 100 years have ranged wildly. One year, the value of the dollar increased by 10.5

percent, while there was 18 percent of *lost* buying-power another. Imagine making a 10 percent return and being able to buy 8 percent less than when you started!

For most of the twentieth century, the value of the dollar bounced back and forth, and the average inflation annually over that same 100 years was 3.3 percent. However, from 1973–1982, the average rate of inflation or lost buying power was 8.75 percent per year. Since then, it has been much steadier, around 2.5 percent. Who is to say this steady control will continue? What are the odds that the value of the dollar will be tested in the next ten years?

Nixon untethered the value of the dollar to gold and tied it to oil back in 1971 by demanding that OPEC (Organization of the Petroleum Exporting Countries) could only sell oil for dollars. Inflation rates suddenly moved up along with the cost of oil, starting in 1974, his last year in office. Now the threat of oil being acquired in currencies other than so-called "petrodollars" seems to trigger military action. Currency markets have been far from stable, complicated by plummeting oil prices that keep inflation numbers mostly low, while some costs of living continue to climb.

Someone might instead choose to do something else with retirement money than gamble in the "market." The only certain thing is change, so whatever conclusions drawn from the past may have little or no relevance in the future. For example, a future without dollar dominancy is certainly possible and could have dire consequences.

One way to encourage the local or global circulation of money in a predictable and evenhanded way would be to create a financial system in which money loses value over time if not spent or invested. Maximum value would be realized by use, rather than by accumulation. Later, we will discuss the potential of local and business-to-business currencies, now so easy to introduce through the Internet, but difficult to tax and regulate.

Regardless of how currencies will fluctuate in the future, the stock market as we know it should be viewed skeptically. I will consider how this could change in Part II. Assuming money is being invested in "the market," however, matching dollars from a business provides a definite advantage. Every dollar earned doubles with the match. In 1992, I missed that one.

Benjamin Franklin's Virtues: Frugality

"Make no expense but to do good to others or yourself, i.e., waste nothing."

"Waste not, want not" is yet another wise saying attributed to Ben Franklin. Commenting on our "throwaway" society, the environmentalist Julia Butterfly Hill asks a haunting question: "Where is 'away'?"[19] We know intuitively that as everything piles up in the dump, there is a hidden future cost. "Zero Waste" companies are taking over municipal waste management in hundreds of U.S. towns and cities and making residents pay up front for every bag of waste. Residents immediately become frugal and cut their waste in half. This is an example of "making no expense" in the first place.

Franklin was also a proponent of saving money—after all, "a penny saved is a penny earned." But frugality, surprisingly, is less about setting money aside and more about expending it to "do good to others or yourself." In this way, by meting out our money for as much good as possible, we will maximize our efficiency and "waste nothing."

CHAPTER 3:

GOING FOR BROKE (1992–1996)

"Give the best that you have to the best that you know." —Hiram "Harry" Bingham IV

In 1992, I was invited to accompany a summer tour to Peru, where I reconnected with the legacy of my grandfather, the explorer who discovered the ruins of Machu Picchu in 1911. On this trip I also met, for the first time, the indigenous people of Peru and learned about their ritualistic sense of the connection between spirit and matter.

Upon my return, a consultant friend introduced me to a bio-healthcare start-up that needed a fundraiser, and soon I was in the office of my first fully for-profit "socially responsible" venture. I was forty-three and quite aware that I had no retirement plan. The only way I could see growing a sum that would support Jenny and me in our old age was to become an entrepreneur. I did not want an office job with a 401(k) and assumed it was too late for that anyway.

At the time, I had no idea that nine out of ten businesses fail early on—even with venture capital, three out of four fail.[20] Nor did I have a clue about the proverbial three-legged stool required for success in almost anything: (1) a winning concept, (2) hard-working and talented management, and (3) enough resources—usually meaning enough money—to reach the finish line.

In the interview process, I presented myself as a person who knew how to write grants and who happened to have friends and family with resources who trusted me. The company was starving for operating capital. The inventor appeared to be a genius, the CEO promised me the world, and I was blinded by the light of all the possibilities. I liked the idea of writing and using the telephone to raise money rather than going door to door. So I first reworked the business plan with my fundraising and writing skills. Next I began warm-calling likely candidates from the Investor's Circle directory, which I shared with my brother Tony. This was the beginning of my association with an extraordinary group of socially minded investors that has lasted for more than twenty years now.

Before I knew it, I was investing time, money, and other resources in the venture, while putting relationships at risk by promoting something that might never succeed. Every entrepreneur must commit themselves in this whole-hearted way, and, though it works out financially only for a few, it is essential for driving innovation. Without such risk takers, the world would not evolve. Let's call it a gift.

The company offered enthralling new technology: a way of solving health issues simply by rearranging amino acids into virtual needles to pierce cell walls, dissolving unhealthy cells and stimulating healthy cells. The research results were awesome, patents were issued, and universities around the world were eager to study this biological breakthrough. I brought in enough investors to limp along and wrote a few successful federal grants, but we still could not find strategic partners to put up serious money despite the promising results.

The initial tests implied that our product had the potential to make a dent in the repeat business of many large pharmaceutical companies that prescribe drugs that do not cure disease, but only take away symptoms. Upon reflection, this may have been one reason why large investors and potential strategic partners chose not to fund us. Once cured, a patient need not buy more. At the time I pushed aside this concern, as well as the worry that Genetically Modified Organisms (GMOs) such as these patented peptide chains might have negative ramifications. Instead I pushed enthusiastically, even when there was no money to pay me.

When funds got tight, I began to work for nothing without demanding equity ownership. What did I know about such seemingly egoistic negotiations? I trusted people at their word. As it turned out, the CEO had overpromised equity to many minor contributors anyway. When I woke up and took my leave of the company after three years, a friend persuaded me to demand stock. I received a handful of shares as back pay and left with a pile of credit card debt. I failed to sell these shares when the market was most ripe. And each time there was an infusion of capital or a strategic merger, the original stock was watered down until it became virtually worthless, despite the potential value of the underlying science.

As happens so often, early investors (known as "angels," probably because of their naïve good will) find themselves elbowed out as venture capitalists (often referred to as "vultures," circling to feed on carnage) or larger, well-funded companies take control. The competitive culture of social Darwinism in business has embittered many otherwise well-intentioned investors, who then avoid taking financial risks despite their desire to do good in the world. I suggest ways to change this culture in the second and third parts of this book.

Benjamin Franklin's Virtues: Industry

"Lose no time, be always employed in something useful. Cut off unnecessary actions!"

Benjamin Franklin, the inventor of "just in time" manufacturing with his printing press franchises, accomplished so much in his life because of his ability to "make haste slowly." His rhyme "a stitch in time saves nine" advocates an alternative to both procrastination and compulsive workaholism. Industry requires focus in order to be most efficient. Successful people who work hard and work smart employ the power of concentration and the concentration of power. Salesmanship literature is full of motivational mantras oriented around conceiving, believing, and achieving sales goals.

In *The Success System That Never Fails*, Napoleon Hill and W. Clement Stone concluded that only three essentials are required for success: "definiteness of purpose" (a concentrated goal), a "positive mental attitude" (concentration on the positive), and a willingness to "go the extra mile" (concentrated effort).[21] All are characteristic of industry and industrious people.

Johann Wolfgang von Goethe is often credited with the saying "Boldness has genius, magic, and power in it." I like the way his scientific archivist, Rudolf Steiner, turned this around: "Genius is a result of industry." To look like a genius, concentrate on a single goal and work harder than anyone else to achieve that goal. Say no to distractions, and say yes to what is most needed.

Once prices reflect real costs and real benefits, investment styles will no longer need to be labeled as "socially responsible" or "impact investing." Each industry will be invested in for its potential to meet human needs in the best possible way—*losing no time, employed always in something useful, and cutting off unnecessary actions!* These focused, efficient enterprises will reward investors as well. Doing well and doing good become more aligned when linked with the genius of industry to solve the key problems of our time.

CHAPTER 4:

GOING FOR BROKE AGAIN (1996–2000)

"Resources that are appreciated
appreciate in value." —Lynne Twist

Allowing credit card debt to grow year by year is not something I would recommend, even if you can manage without having to pay interest as I learned to do. Over the years I had watched other entrepreneurs with stacks of credit cards and, like them, I took advantage of every zero interest offer, religiously paying the minimum each month and moving the growing balance to a new card at the end of every grace period. My credit rating remained excellent, but the burden of debt kept growing.

Nevertheless, in the summer of 1996 Jenny and I decided to splurge. After I left the bio-health firm, we drove 10,000 miles with our youngest son and his dog to explore the natural wonders of this country and to find a Waldorf high school and a new home. We returned east and finally chose Kimberton, Pennsylvania, for its lush greenery and growing social consciousness. New Century Bank was in conception, and I was drawn to its idealistic goal of keeping money local.

In the mornings, I taught lessons to eighth-grade Waldorf students for very little pay so my son could attend tuition-free. I also helped a bit with marketing for the bank. I eventually decided to start my own venture fund, hoping to diversify and reduce risk. As it turned out, the first venture that came to my attention quickly became all-consuming.

The inventor, Janice Archbold, is a brilliant woman who had

a fantastic vision of using the Internet not just as an information highway, but also as a workflow highway. Janice's father had developed the first computer for the Pentagon, and by her early twenties she was setting up corporate systems all around the country, including the Big Board on Wall Street. When Three Mile Island failed years later, she was called in to solve the facility's systems problem.

She became determined to solve the white-collar unemployment problem of the early 1990s by matching remote workers with work, first through 800 numbers and later through the Internet. After applying for broad patents, she went on the road to no avail—I think because she was too smart and made investors feel their intellectual limitations. She was the kind of smart, socially minded entrepreneur I wanted to help.

I became the face of the organization and acted as Janice's liaison. My job was to translate her complex and detailed invention into layman's terms that investors and strategic partners could understand. We soon had the backing of a powerful venture fund and put together a team. I began paying off my credit cards little by little and no longer needed to teach to keep my son in school. I realized with this second technology company that I had a gift for understanding complex ideas and enjoyed putting them forward in a form people could understand.

At this time, Jenny found new work helping women transition to life outside of a group home. Jenny, our youngest son, and I moved into a shared mansion with four women recovering from emotional breakdowns. This was easy compared to our early community work, and the free room and board allowed me to pay down the rest of my debt.

I was able to develop commercial interest from a number of corporations. They had signed nondisclosure agreements, but were learning enough about our systems to be dangerous. Then in 1999 our lead investor stopped the flow of funding, theoretically until the patents were issued, afraid we might give away our "secret sauce."

Suddenly without either debt or financial resources, I took some time off to reflect and explore my purpose in life, relying on some small research jobs, coaching tennis, and guiding people to Peru. During these trips in the Andes, I rediscovered the meaning of ritual and the great relief and joy I felt in experiencing the close relationship between spirit and matter. I celebrated my fiftieth birthday in April 2000 on Lake Titicaca, the highest navigable lake in the world. That night, when all the visible planets aligned with the sun and moon, I decided to explore a religious vocation. When we returned, I made arrangements to study at a seminary in Stuttgart, Germany, thinking I could sell the stock from my first venture if I ran out of money. Looking back, this was somehow an essential part of my financial journey.

In Germany, I recognized that despite the meaningfulness of a religious path, I was not "called" to work with one congregation at a time any more than with one classroom at a time. I wanted to connect with something that would make a difference on a global scale, something like the transformation of money.

Leaving after the first semester, I returned home to face the humbling fact that I needed a job, preferably a meaningful one. I put on a tie and went to a job fair with no clear idea of what I would find or what I wanted. I had nothing to sell; I went just to see whom I was drawn to and who seemed drawn to me.

My head was spinning in the cavernous space full of cacophonous chatter. I visited only two booths and met two different gentlemen who happened to represent the world of finance. Two interviews followed in the next days. When I told the first that I was undecided about returning to the seminary, he ushered me out the door without hesitation. My next interview was at Legg Mason, an investment management firm. When I made the same comment to the second gentleman, who happened to be a Yalie and a tennis player like me, he took a risk and told me:

1. His company realized that socially responsible investing was the coming thing;

2. I was just the sort of person he was looking to hire; and

3. He was confident I would love working with Legg Mason!

That fall I studied and passed the Series 7 and 65 exams required to become a licensed financial advisor. Suddenly I was a stockbroker with a nice title: financial advisor.

To justify this move into what I had always considered the evil empire or the belly of the beast, I developed the idea that the transactions of the marketplace could become a sacred ritual. Even the stock market could theoretically become a place for measuring human values, where prices could rise or fall based on the perceived benefit to humanity. I learned that the friends and family who had supported my three earlier ventures were unhappy with their investment portfolios, and that some were actively seeking new ways to invest. Maybe I could help. But first I had a great deal to learn.

Benjamin Franklin's Virtues: Moderation

"Avoid extremes; forbear resenting injuries so much as you think they deserve."

Detractors in his day accused Franklin of being a polytheist, a believer in many gods. Actually, he practiced moderation and balance, forbearing resentment against those who disagreed with him. In Franklin's conversation circles, which grew into international scientific collaborations, participants had to leave their grievances at the door and were fined for interrupting others or directly disagreeing. For Franklin, moderation was a central discipline. How can this virtue be applied to the world of money?

Instead of resenting competition, ethical individualists can moderate their competitive zeal while maintaining their uniqueness and competitive edge. These captains of the future are learning to serve everyone's best interests by forming symbiotic relationships with other diverse companies. Everyone wins.

Avoiding extremes is a discipline investors need to reduce the zigzagging volatility, or swings, of the public markets. Fear enters the picture with the worry that something might go wrong. Once concerns become obsessive, investors tend to stagnate in indecision and withdraw their money from circulation and keep it under the mattress. Even if we care deeply about our world, fear may keep us from taking action.

Moderation of *inaction* is as important, if not more important, than the moderation of action. Some risk, some letting go, some engagement in the flow of the economy is always healthy. If losses occur, and they inevitably will, the ability to "forbear resentment" is required to benefit in the long run if value is being created.

Passion, rather than compassion, can easily lead one into the dangerous waters of greed. Even the most ethical investors can be seduced by risky "one-off" investments that have appeal because of the chance to get rich while doing good. Any single investment carries a risk of failure, even if the product or service is brilliant.

The investor must feel secure in the present and future, including the future of the planet. Equally important is the need to grow resources for future dreams. In simple financial terms, this boils down to moderation between income and growth: the rudder and sail of every investment journey.

CHAPTER 5:

ESCAPING THE BROKERAGE DRAGON (2000–2011)

"Not everything that counts can be counted, and not everything that can be counted counts."
—*Sign hanging in Einstein's office at Princeton*

MUTUAL FUNDS

Working with other people's money made sense to me for many reasons. Unlike most of the new financial advisors in my "class" who were put to work cold-calling from phonebooks, I had already established a network of supporters who had trusted me through the funding of three ventures. None of them felt that the rest of their financial portfolios was invested in companies that truly reflected their values. These investors did not want the best of the worst (often referred to as "best of class"), like the most ethical oil company, but wanted to invest in companies that were making a positive difference in the world.

Nevertheless, in order to avoid excessive risk, I had to persuade them to compromise their values a bit for the sake of diversification and invest in imperfect mutual funds while I developed my own list of appropriate stocks. Like most new brokers, I faced the daunting challenge of developing enough of a following to support myself as the firm slowly weaned me off my salary.

Buying individual stocks for others takes either mindless bravado or tremendous courage. I saw former college athletes pushing risky stocks to their old teammates, sometimes winning big for a while before tanking and leaving the firm.

Avoid brokers who rely on your willingness to pay commission on each sale, because their incentive to trade may not always be in your best interest. There are, however, ethical brokers who trade only occasionally, and one may argue that this works out to be less expensive than set advisory fees. These fees are often charged year after year with essentially little change in the portfolio.

The more conservative brokers who trade individual stocks depend entirely on analysts who have the time and resources to get to know companies well. Because my father taught me to look at things "upside down and backwards," I wondered if I could discover "off the wall street" companies, as I called them—companies not followed by analysts but that have great stories. My courage and confidence were boosted altogether too much with my first stock pick, which went up 2,000 percent in two years.

This pick, the best-performing stock in that ten-year period, was Hanson Natural Soda, whose Blue Sky brand was carried by Whole Foods and Trader Joe's. While Trader Joe's was private, Whole Foods stock was overpriced, selling at more than twenty-five times what the company was currently earning. Meanwhile, Hanson was priced at five times earnings.

Most professional investors assume that if you multiply the number of shares held by a company times the stock price and divide by fifteen to get the current earnings, the stock price would be fairly valued. Below that mean value, the stock would be considered a "value stock," above it "overvalued," or, if growing with momentum, a "growth stock." This norm is one of the cultural assumptions of the strange ritual we have developed called the "Market."

From 2001 to 2002, the average price of S&P 500 stocks in relation to earnings was at least twenty-five (in the same range as the market in 2015). This meant that most stocks, including Whole Foods, were overvalued. The tiny but growing company called Hansen Natural Soda, with a price that was only five times the earnings at the time, was a significantly undervalued "value stock." I had noticed their Blue Sky Soda was the only soda at that time on the shelf at both Whole Foods and Trader Joe's. I felt the company would surely benefit by the astounding growth of these two retailers, so I acquired it for all my clients.

A 2002 article about Hansen in the *Wall Street Journal* soon caused its share price to double and double and split. (A "split" is when a share is issued for each share owned because the price is too high to believe.) It continued on in this way, growing exponentially in two years. Eventually I learned that, in addition to "natural" soda, Hanson produced Monster, a highly caffeinated energy drink. I decided to get out, taking a handsome profit for my clients.

Although realizing this experience was perhaps beginner's luck, I was still encouraged to look outside the boxed-in universe that I saw in almost every prospective client's portfolio. The same stocks were weighted heavily, with many different mutual funds owning the same stocks. Following the majority, and listening to the same commentators and analysts and wholesalers, seemed to me inherently risky. The phrase "a high tide lifts all boats" applies equally to the low tides, so I wanted to find a deep cove away from the marina.

Unfortunately, brokerage firms do not make this easy for advisors. Each firm has a limited list of managers allowed on its platform (the "stable") and have agreements with only certain analysts, each of which only follow a relatively small selection of stocks. Emerging managers with fresh ideas and unheard-of stocks are largely off-limits. Many public companies (more than 60,000 globally), like Hansen, are hard to purchase without paperwork and permissions.

Certainly the status quo feels safer as boats rise and fall together, but my question was, "What is the value of these advisors if they all follow the same course of action?" They may have been better at holding their client's hand, but their work was often neither original nor truly customized. This bothered me, especially since the common theme in all marketing was "performance." The reality I observed was that:

1. The best managers in any five-year period tend to be in the middle or worse in the next five. (They've already taken their profits and often run out of steam.)

2. The average active manager, trying to beat the market by picking the best stocks, actually underperforms the market once fees are accounted for.

3. Most investors underperform mutual funds by coming in late on a growth spurt and leaving in disbelief on a downturn.

Investors interested in "performance" still want "in," despite the disclaimer that past performance is not indicative of future performance. This principle applies equally to "socially responsible" funds. I was at Legg Mason in the heyday of Bill Miller, who broke all records by beating the S&P 500 fifteen years in a row. This was unheard of. Despite his brilliance, much of his success could be attributed to his troupe of advisors who flowed new cash to him every month. He could risk buying stocks at lower and lower valuations as they slid downward—then, like magic, when they popped back up, he made unusual gains. As soon as all the advisors, including me, were shipped off to Citigroup Smith Barney in 2006, Miller's cash cow reversed. His performance quickly went from best to worst.

BIG BANKS

In early 2006, most of the Legg Mason advisors were invited to a big hotel to be feted by Citigroup. It was one of the last occasions Sanford "Sandy" Weill held forth as chairman of what was then the largest corporation in the world in terms of "impact" (not necessarily "positive impact"). I excitedly assumed I could use these resources to offer more investment choices to my clients at Legg Mason. In fact, the opposite was true.

Tight, bureaucratic, and impersonal, the conference turned my stomach when the speaker leaned out like a snake oil salesman and said, "You are going to make so much money on mortgages!" He offered $2,000 for each mortgage application turned in—even if the mortgage was not realized. Jaws dropped, and brokers grinned. Something was amiss, but they just wanted paper. Little did I know that the company needed "paper," even worthless paper, to justify the debt on its balance sheets. This was the beginning of what could have been the end of big banks.

Six months later, on top of the unethical mortgage push, I noticed that interest rates on cash in my clients' portfolios differed for no apparent reason. Clients with higher fees earned higher interest rates. Older folks, whose fees were minimal, lost yield in their cash. I was mortified and decided to get out when I realized that Citi was following Merrill Lynch's business model of manipulating interest rates to improve the bottom line. How could I submit SRI clients to this amoral manipulation? I took a big risk by leaving the comfort of a big corporation, but found I still had a great deal to learn.

Turning down a substantial offer from Morgan Stanley for my "book of business," I decided to join an independent Registered Investment Advisor (RIA) for free. My new partner believed in passive index investing and had recently set up an SRI index for U.S. stocks. He was convinced that despite my "good luck" as a stock picker, all that really mattered "at the end of the day" (a phrase that now makes me wary) was "asset allocation"—the portfolio's proportions of cash, fixed income, and equities. These are broken down into smaller subgroups and further diversified by size, industry, geography, etc.

In the business of finance, the common understanding at that time was that 92 percent of portfolio performance depended on how it was weighted (small versus big, tech versus industrial, and so on); 6 percent on the underlying companies picked; and 2 percent on timing. Nowadays, monster computers do most of the trading in tiny fractions of a second, giving institutional investors a significant advantage over those who pick stocks based on their own calculations.

Regardless of supercomputers, if any part of the world economy is growing quickly and you own none of it, you are unlikely to do as well as those who are heavily weighted in that sector, no matter how good a stock picker you are. Changing the weightings in different asset classes was all that seemed to matter. I came to the conclusion that, if true, this would hold good for a universe of positive investments just as well. Why not build portfolios that are weighted wisely with investments that would have a positive impact on the world?

I proposed building a set of funds, and the RIA's only mandate was that he'd have total control of the day-to-day operations, compliance, and finances. As the thought leader, I would focus on designing and marketing the portfolios. I was relieved to be able to concentrate on my responsibilities and went along with this siloed approach, forgetting about best practices. The founder was a well-known "socially responsible" pioneer and was so confident that I backed off instead of demanding transparency.

We started growing relatively quickly, and while preparing to reallocate my clients' investments in 2007, we sold our overvalued stocks. We were happy to have been 60 percent in cash at the start of that year, which turned out to be fortuitous since 2008 was the year of the next market crash. And that year our clients lost, on average, only 5 percent, when most traditional investors lost 30–40 percent. We were off to a great start.

MARGIN/LEVERAGE

In 2008, it was very common for funds to leverage at highly risky levels, sometimes borrowing over 50 percent of the money they used to make investments. Trading firms continue to encourage this as they receive a percentage on all the money borrowed and very little on the money they trade. Individual brokers did the same for their clients in separately managed accounts by setting up "margin" accounts to borrow extra money, like borrowing extra chips at the casino.

A seasoned broker had advised me to read the fine print and to avoid highly leveraged funds, as a bad investment would only be that much worse if you couldn't pay back what was borrowed. I also suspected that bogus mortgage paper was backing many of these loans.

Of course leverage works well when you do well, accelerating your winnings, but at what risk? Credit cards are no different really; you borrow money to invest in yourself, maybe to become better dressed and more impressive so life seems better or bigger. In the end, the margin can get "called" as creditors demand money you don't have, and suddenly you are caught in financial embarrassment, drowned in debt.

I did not know when I joined that the owner was deeply leveraged. His indebtedness had started years earlier in the mid-nineties, long before I met him, and accelerated after a suddenly plummeting currency caught him off-guard and destroyed his investments. I realized years later that he must have been too proud to file for bankruptcy and simply had borrowed more and more from idealistic friends to pay interest. His blind spot was entitlement: he believed he deserved it and that all would work out for him one day. He encouraged me to join him without fully informing me of this situation.

Since that time I have known how critical it is to insist on best practices of openness and transparency. Instead I enjoyed the simplicity of zero bureaucracy alongside someone with a ton of experience. "Often wrong but never in doubt" was his affable refrain. He enabled me to build my dream portfolios while keeping me siloed away from what he was doing. He was caught in an audit and eventually lost his license. In 2011 the company was shut down, and I had to start over with those clients who still believed in my integrity and our common vision.

You can imagine the anger and frustration when clients who opted out could not get all their money right away. Had everyone simply stayed invested, regular payouts of income would not have been a problem. Some of the investments have taken longer than expected to return principal and interest, but not outside a normal scope for these kinds of innovative private debt instruments. There have been no defaults since we reorganized, and the new loan fund alone has been returning close to 7 percent while departing investors are waiting for payouts. But for them, this may be beside the point.

The financial industry is full of such stories. When a person gets too deep in debt to see a way out, they may become numb and drift into a mindless state of denial, seeing no harm in taking more and more until they get caught. The phrase "drowning in debt" has taken on a new meaning for me. My earliest childhood memory is of nearly drowning after I plunged off a diving board into the dark pool of the Brook, a swimming hole on our Connecticut farm. I remember blissfully staring up at the sun from the bottom, and peacefully watching my bubbles floating to the surface before my eight-year-old cousin rudely tackled me, dragged my three-year-old body onto the bank, and roughly pumped me out.

In this case, those who were exposed to the malfeasance also experienced the rude awakening along with the debtor. In reaction to the harm done to me and to my clients, I experienced all the stages of grief: denial, anger, bargaining, depression, and acceptance. In 2012, I took charge, along with a newly configured team of workers dedicated to fixing what we could and saving the best investments. Our goal was to prove that, over time, all clients, disgruntled or not, would realize that working with us had become beneficial.

A wise mentor once told me that life will never throw you anything you can't handle: the challenges of life would not be there but for your capacity to overcome them. The most difficult professional challenge I have had to endure was facing my shortcomings and the anger of friends. I chose to make amends by building the best team I could possibly lead. In April of 2012, the newly established Scarab Funds launched; in 2013 the team was strengthened by the addition of extraordinary advisors, consultants, and professional money managers, including four MBAs, an MA in History, a PhD, and two BAs: one in Finance and International Business and the other in Mathematics. I am now surrounded by brilliant and pedigreed people!

In closing this chapter, I would like to note that the passive investing trend has mostly been usurped by the most active trading practices in history. The big institutional funds make more than 500 trades per second. Since I began fourteen years ago, the average holding period for stocks has dwindled from years to months to hours and may reach the maximum "efficiency" when held only for a fraction of a second.

Certainly human conceptions of qualitative value are not deeply considered in the algorithms that run most of the trading in the public marketplace. One cannot even fathom what is happening, much less impose conscious human values. Our faithful clients, despite the shock from the former principal's malfeasance, still believed in our values and long-term prosperity. Rebuilding and continuing this work with them has allowed us to continue developing our understanding of how money works and what matters most as we move into the future.

The need to understand our impact on the world is what inspired me to leave Yale in the first place and to learn to work with my hands, to learn how to take care of stuff. Shortly before making that decision, I read *The Immense Journey* by Loren Eiseley, which makes the argument that our minds differentiate us from the rest of creation, and as we forget how things work, we run the risk of devolving.[22] The only chance to retain our humanity in a world valued by machines is to move to a different "universe." This is the theme of Part 2.

PART II:

WHAT WE CAN DO

CHAPTER 6:
MAKING A PLAN

*"This may sound too simple, but is great in consequence.
Until one is committed, there is hesitancy, the chance to draw
back, always ineffectiveness. Concerning all acts of
initiative (and creation), there is one elementary truth
the ignorance of which kills countless ideas and splendid plans:
that the moment one definitely commits oneself, the providence
moves too. A whole stream of events issues from the decision,
raising in one's favor all manner of unforeseen incidents,
meetings and material assistance, which no
man could have dreamt would have come his way."*
—*W. H. Murray in* The Scottish Himalaya Expedition, *1951*

"Boldness has genius, magic, and power in it."
—*Popularly attributed to Goethe*

Although my focus so far has been on the stock market, this is clearly not the only way to make a difference with money. In fact, the stock market, which plays so strongly on our short-term reactive emotions of greed and fear, may be the least direct and most distracting way to invest. On the other hand, it remains geopolitically like the tail that wags the dog. For investors who are looking for long-term growth, the main benefit of the stock market is liquidity: getting cash out by selling stocks can be done easily and quickly.

When investing in the stock market, a conscious investor must first consider whether to invest in harmful companies, in hopes of having some influence over their business practices, or whether to divest from the "bad actors" completely. The end goal of the second approach is to encourage other investors to improve the valuation of good companies that need support, while diminishing the demand and therefore the stock value of the bad ones.

Activist investors, per se, are not necessarily socially responsible. Warren Buffet and Carl Icahn own enough shares in companies to earn seats on the board and influence decisions, but their focus is solely on money. Representatives of SRI mutual funds attend meetings with business executives and certainly have received increasing support from other investors; still, their impact is hard to measure. It is also hard to imagine that their influence is greater than the Icahns and Buffets of the world.

Over the years, companies have opted to meet with social activists rather than expose themselves to the PR inferno of heated proxy battles. As long as stockholders expect companies to do solely what is best for the financial bottom line, these discussions will remain mostly talk. Most of the compromise seems to be on the SRI side of the table, according to Harvard fellow Heather White:

> Corporations have increasingly persuaded their non-profit critics to join drawn-out discussions called engagements or worse, *partnerships*. The critics get a sense of influence, and in return they promise not to embarrass the firms publicly in the future—regardless of the outcome of the engagement. Many advocacy groups now sign confidentiality agreements or accept money from previously targeted corporations to monitor *improvements* being made. The results are rarely made public.[23]

This is why 350.org, a campaign to convince endowments to divest from fossil fuels, follows the same path that freed Nelson Mandela from jail: divestment. When activist investors refuse to invest or do business with bad corporations, it has an immediate impact. Skeptics might argue that someone else trying to make money will simply buy the stock instead, so what difference does it make? The answer is straightforward: the market reflects cultural beliefs and emotions. With enough momentum, unpopular companies and industries will trend downwards. Investors in SRI should embolden managers to end their engagements with harmful companies and focus more energy on finding and funding new solutions. This is a critical factor to consider when choosing an advisor or fund manager.

Fixating on money for money's sake will always lead to the vicissitudes of fear and greed. No matter how socially minded you are, keeping a long-term outlook without being distracted by current dips and rises in financial values is difficult. Supporting beneficial enterprises is gratifying, but most people are too busy to keep track of rapidly changing markets, and the watchful eyes of an advisor or consultant can be essential. Nevertheless, you will need both practical and emotional intelligence for the journey. A financial plan at least provides you with a theoretical roadmap to guide your decisions.

If you ask financial advisors, consultants, or financial planners to share their ideas for positive impact and the common good, they might look at you and respond, "Listen, Charlie, one day you just have to decide between the money and the trees!" Or, "No one has asked me for that before." Do start asking, and don't be shy; every consultant and planner should know the lexicon and provide you with options. In fact, financial advisors should be *initiating* the conversation on envisioning and investing in a better future. Here are a few points to consider before investing.

First, decide how much you are comfortable losing. That's right. Some of this amount could just be given away or spent on personal development, such as education and training; alternatively, it could be invested in a responsible and potentially profitable business. This kind of private equity/venture option used to be reserved for so-called "accredited" investors. Millionaires beyond the value of their homes, these investors were supposedly sophisticated enough to lose their own money! Now many unaccredited investors are allowed to take chances as well. Depending on your state, "crowdfunding," built into the JOBS Act of 2011, allows private ventures to be publicized for any investors, whether accredited or not.[24]

Of course, for a more indirect impact with far less risk, hundreds of SRI stock funds are available, offering a broad range of choice amongst public companies. Using this portfolio approach, you can plan for growth in the years ahead with easy exits, if and when cash is needed. Beware, however, *no one can guarantee these funds will go up*! And the companies that appear under the aegis of SRI may surprise you—some are quite willing to invest in industries that you may consider harmful.

I am on the board of CSRHub a technology firm that allows users to compare companies based on a variety of aggregated data points, including data from environmental, social, and governance ratings firms.[25] Before buying a mutual fund, an investor can check out how the specific companies measure up. Similarly, a sister operation we developed, WikiPositive, provides details about many companies—what is positive about their business models, what it is they claim, and what inherent controversies may exist.[26] The goal is to eventually develop a global intelligent mob that posts and updates lists of positive initiatives, rosters of experts in different fields, and geographies. These resources can be tapped for deeper "due diligence," the formal deep digging required for making any prudent investment. There is more on these two websites in the next chapter.

If you do happen to be an accredited investor with $1–5 million in investable assets, or better, a qualified investor with more than $5 million to invest, and you are looking for colleagues to help identify positive impact venture deals, a growing number of organizations like Investors' Circle or Toniic have local chapters in a number of cities.[27,28] Online resources include Maximpact, an organization that chooses established fund managers to vet social enterprises, and Mission Markets, which has positioned itself as the go-to site for connecting investors with positive investment opportunities.[29,30]

Second, consider how much regular income you need to withdraw from your portfolio. This money can be invested in well-secured loans with a range of interest rates and time spans. Kiva is one highly successful site that matches small-scale investors with $25 or more to invest with small micro-entrepreneurs in the "majority" or "developing" world.[31] Investors can expect to get money back to recycle, but interest does not accrue in the meantime. If income is needed from this part of your investment strategy, consider purchasing a certificate of deposit in a local community bank.

For greater impact and higher yields, private debt funds are taking shape and getting attention. Investors who consider themselves good judges of character and are willing to tolerate more risk might lend money directly to a trusted social entrepreneur. Just be sure to have a clear understanding in place. You should find out whether the social entrepreneur is qualified as a "B" Corporation, with a proven commitment to the common good, or at least a member of the BALLE network (Business Alliance for Local Living Economies).[32] If you feel a particular connection to the land, you can turn to another burgeoning group, Slow Money, which has local chapters around the country, or look into Community Supported Agriculture (CSA).[33,34]

A traditional advisor might allocate this part of the portfolio to a mix of corporate and municipal bonds, including some high-yield bonds. If these bonds are packaged in funds, it is important to realize that when interest rates rise, the funds must lose value. This is especially true if they use leverage (i.e., borrowed money) to increase their exposure to the market.

Because of the current low-yield environment, some are simply looking for more stocks to own that offer high dividends. This is nice, but the risk of the market losing value is high, not to mention the ethical concern that companies might use their profits to buy back shares for management bonuses and paying dividends, instead of spending on R&D for improving their products and services.

Third, consider how much money you can set aside that you *cannot* afford to lose—how much cash is enough for now and later, and how you can best spend it. This guideline is customizable for every individual, family, or institution. Two specific questions help string through all possible considerations: *For each decision I make to spend money, what is the impact of my lifestyle first on those who indirectly serve me through their labor and second on the environment that supports us all?*

Advising investors is a profound responsibility, as much an art as a science, that requires a good deal of emotional intelligence. This is why I enrolled in a training course in Gestalt psychology right after beginning my advisory work. Many advisors are disinclined to "go there," but ways of thinking that consider the client's whole being are becoming more common in the world of finance.

At The Natural Wealth Conservancy, financial planner Mary Carol Rose has created *somatic financial integration*—an educational coaching model that honors "the art of exchange." Each client is taught how to exercise the power of conscious choice through deep engagement with their own unique wealth and connectivity. Mary Carol says it like this: "We need to awaken our imaginative and creative potentials for how wealth is felt, lived, created, and exchanged." Obviously, this approach is only for investors who are interested in heightening their own awareness.

FIXED-INTEREST INCOME, LOANS, NOTES, AND BONDS OF ALL KINDS

With all the financial options available, lending is perhaps the most fulfilling in terms of community and mutual support, yet it has all but dried up as a resource, especially for those with less.

There has been much controversy about the rights and wrongs of charging interest. According to Lewis Hyde in his classic book *The Gift*, the ancient Hebrew people isolated themselves socially by lending freely between themselves while charging interest to "foreigners" outside their tribes.[35] The practice of usury was harshly ostracized from the time of Aristotle, who referred to interest as an illegitimate child—that it was money unnaturally derived from money.

Later, Thomas Aquinas redeemed this previously antisocial practice once the Crusades were draining the Catholic Church's coffers. He justified interest as compensation for allowing someone else to use your resources for a time. Later again, to save the Protestant Reformation, both Luther and Calvin saw the need to justify it as well.

Though Islam still forbids charging interest, it is now tacitly understood that a lender at risk deserves to benefit for the risk taken, but in the form of equity ownership, rather than interest. Despite technical differences, it seems that everyone, unconsciously or consciously, participates in interest-bearing debt, and usury laws are mostly defunct. But many questions remain.

First of all, how much should be charged? Many socially minded investors are quite content with the relatively low returns offered by nonprofits and foundations, which need capital for philanthropic or educational projects. In effect, the investor lends money by only "charging" 0–4 percent or so, and they might be happy just to keep up with inflation if the money is used for a meaningful purpose. This concessionary lending cannot be adopted on a large scale for retirement plans, however, because it will not generate enough for the future retirees to live on.

Pension funds need a return of at least 6 percent to satisfy the future needs of pensioners. For decades, "defined benefits" were offered to employees after they retired. Businesses set aside retirement money, and in keeping with this profound commitment, the fiduciaries of the "pension funds" set aside each year for this purpose carefully invested them in bonds that grew at known rates for known periods of time. Unless there was a serious crash, these bonds could be counted on to deliver what was expected. Gradually, trustees saw fit to venture into the stocks of "blue chip" Dow Jones industrial companies after recognizing that their average growth rates were higher than slow and steady bonds. In the 1990s, pension plans added international stocks, then technology stocks, until everything came tumbling down at the end of the century.

So, seeing that they had perhaps not been so prudent, many corporations changed the defined "benefit" to a defined "contribution" for their pensioners. That meant that they still put aside ("contributed") money for their employees' futures, but with no idea how it will deliver down the road. Perhaps it is time to return to fixed-return plans. The problem, however, is that the privately held Federal Reserve has kept interest rates so low that the benefits might seem too low to be worth saving at all.

This brings up our next question. How is it that the Federal Reserve Bank, a private institution (neither federal, holding any reserves, nor a bank), can decide how many dollars to print and how much interest should be charged between banks? In our current financial system, money seems to be generated out of thin air. Banks borrow against their deposits from other banks, who have borrowed against their own deposits, then borrow more against this newly borrowed money—and so on. Soon the leverage (the percentage of borrowed money versus actual deposits) becomes astronomical, and the debt on the books becomes worthless.

This system is fundamentally not grounded in reality. It is beyond the scope of this book to say more than this: A new money paradigm requires currencies that lose value over time at an unchanging rate. Money would never be stored under the mattress, but would stay valuable by circulating.

The third question: How can we incorporate real lending into a portfolio that will provide sufficient returns for retirement while benefiting society and the environment at the same time? Real lending occurs when real money is provided for real projects that can pay back interest because they are creating real value. Some will take a long time, and so they may have to offer higher interest. Some might be riskier, and should again expect to pay a higher rate. Other philanthropic initiatives may never produce a profit. In this case, the lender would be happy if they simply got their money back to lend again. So, there is a need to differentiate and apply due diligence.

Initiatives with positive impact are as prolific as the number of problems that need to be solved. Below are three case studies from our experience as a fixed-income lender:

Solutions for Progress (SFP), formerly a low-profile think tank, realized that with some research, software development, and a call center, they could partner with NGOs around the country to provide people with information about welfare benefits.[36] With the help of a small, high-interest loan under $2 million from our fund, this organization has helped move over one billion dollars in new benefits to the poor and needy. These benefits consist mostly of Medicaid reimbursements, but also disaster insurance, tax rebates, and other relief programs. From the website: "The products and services offered by SFP are designed to assist individuals in meeting their financial needs both in the short- and long-term and to ultimately become self-sufficient." SFP has been able to manage this high-interest loan because states pay the NGOs to assist people, and the NGOs in turn pay SFP for their support system. Everyone wins! SFP has won a Best for the Planet award from B Corp.

Panel Group is led by the visionary economist Elena Panaritis, the author of *Prosperity Unbound*, who persuaded the World Bank to allow her to develop and implement a technique for formalizing land values in Peru. The $60 million project took many years, but many regard this as responsible for the country's unprecedented economic turnaround. Aware that 70 percent of real estate in the world is not formally owned, Panel Group has taken lessons learned in Peru to Eastern Europe, where a great deal of former government real estate is now occupied without proper title. The expectation is that land values in each municipality will increase, just as land values in Peru went up tenfold once a system was in place that could be trusted by local lenders. A proprietary financial arrangement designed by Panaritis allows the lenders to harvest interest and possibly an "equity kicker" should each project go smoothly.

Anthurium Solutions developed out of a desire to match idle, intelligent workers with work by using the Internet as a "workflow highway," not just an "information highway."[37] (See Chapter 4.) Remotely matching intelligent caregivers with patients while seamlessly linking information and workflow, Anthurium prevents waste and provides a new level of personalized attention to the healing process. Angel investors bootstrapped this start-up, which owns valuable, proven patents. The patent's valuation increased the unproven company's price tag, deterring predatory venture capitalists. This called for "venture debt": high-yielding loans that accumulate interest while the investors wait for a potentially significant return of capital. (Full disclosure: I am a 5 percent owner of Anthurium at the time of this writing.)

All three cases demonstrate how relatively small amounts of capital are needed for developing breakthrough innovations with major positive impact. Though in aggregate such projects could attract large amounts of capital, the problem is that each of them is isolated and requires distinct attention and expertise. On the other hand, with enough goodwill in the world, more fund managers will package similar opportunities so that larger institutional funds can benefit from the financial return and social or environmental impact. This will happen if investors are given access to an easily searchable list of due-diligence experts vetting projects globally. Developing diversified private-loan portfolios takes courage and collaboration, but due diligence becomes easier with the help of experts around the world available to confirm the worthiness of each enterprise. Likewise, for our money to make a global difference while meeting long-term needs, we need financial advisors who are linked to such networks of expertise.

Each person has dreams and goals that, without a plan, go mostly unrealized. The meaning of John Lennon's lyric that "life is what happens to you while you're busy making plans" is well taken: We do not know the future, and so living in the present is where life "happens." Yet we can create a context for our life plan and with every transaction express what matters most.

Unfortunately, because of wild stock market rides, the Great Recession, and unclear planning, many in the Boomer generation may die in poverty, supported in part by Medicaid. In the wealthiest nation on earth, economists expect more than half of all Americans to live in poverty before age sixty-five, and many more afterward. We need to plan our journey and make sure we don't get stuck on a highway to the wrong destination!

COOKIE-CUTTER ASSET ALLOCATION

Oddly enough, most investors' poor knowledge of their specific financial situations is often shared by their financial advisors, who are almost always good-looking, personable, and—perhaps most important—discrete. Individual recipes for "allocating assets" may appear highly personalized, but in practice, the allocation is more often derived from automatic formulas and simple forms. The "financial advisor" may even have negligible understanding of the design of each client's portfolio. Financial advisors tend to be personally close to their clients—and are sometimes even trained to show up at weddings and funerals. But they will never disclose that their secret sauce is typically developed in the back office out of simple templates.

In fact, asset allocation often follows a cookie-cutter formula that only changes according to a client's income needs and level of risk aversion. The advisor provides just the right proportions to make the client feel comfortable and then divides up the money to "experts" in each asset class. Those "experts" in turn know how to construct a fund in their particular asset class, but may know next to nothing about the actual investments, relying entirely on their analysts on the next level down.

For example, if the asset class is something simple like "large-cap domestic," macro-level expertise is needed to construct the portfolio with the best current proportions of the various industries in the U.S. economy. But the representative stocks for each industry are chosen based on the analysis of *other* experts. This dependence on more and more detailed expertise is what keeps everyone in the dark. There is an appearance of meticulous order, that everything is "in place," but it hides a serious lack of awareness. The reason so few investors do better than others is because all are more or less dependent on the same experts at the same time. The supercomputers have already "been there, done that" even before the crowd moves to the next obvious opportunity.

Significant problems arise from this systematic approach. When unexpected "black swan" events occur, investors move in packs, like lemmings stampeding over a cliff, which exaggerates the movement of valuations. Suddenly, a very ordered algorithmic world is triggered into chaos. Why risk having such a large portion of your assets stranded on the Wall Street highway?

Benjamin Franklin's Virtues: Order

"Let all your things have their places; let each part of your business have its time."

People who have their affairs "in order" inevitably become masters of their money. Benjamin Franklin certainly was. It is awesome to see the order and beauty of his handwritten ledger in black ink from a feather quill, with no smudges and rarely any crossed-out items, each page full and just under three feet wide! His illegitimate son sided with the British during the Revolutionary War and was given large tracts of land in New Jersey by the king. Years later, Ben got out the accounts of every penny he had ever loaned his son and reckoned he would have to pay it back in land, which he did!

The discipline of having everything "in place and on time" is essential for investors. Knowing what you own and being able to stand behind your portfolio is essential for conscious investment success.

CHAPTER 7:

WHAT'S HAPPENING NOW

*"Rather than a country of rugged individuals,
we can be a country of rugged communities." —Judy Wicks*

As described in the last chapter, the biggest problem facing impact investors today is that *most advisors only have a small universe from which to choose.* Each brokerage house or retirement plan has selling agreements with only certain mutual funds—or, for institutional clients, their own stable of private managers. Advisors interested in overlooked public companies are met with resistance, and retail investors find it next to impossible to make sanctioned private investments. The result is that advisors all pass on similar information to clients, and investment portfolios look startlingly similar. Instead of choosing investments from the 60,000+ public companies globally providing a broad range of diversification, even the largest sovereign funds exist in a limited universe.

This landscape is changing, thanks to the availability of information on the Internet, and do-it-yourself stock jockeys are riding the ups and downs of the market without advice, for better or worse. A number of alternative initiatives are maturing outside the stock market, while others are still in the incubation stage.

THE LOCALIST MOVEMENT

One such multifaceted initiative is the burgeoning "localist" movement, which is turning its back on the stock market altogether. This approach slows down expectations by developing the local economy without worrying so much about the rest. Since the turn of the millennium, the "local living economy" idea has taken off, fostering all kinds of small sustainable business organizations in over ninety cities.

A perfect example is the Business Alliance for Local Living Economies (BALLE), which was conceived in 2001 by Judy Wicks and Laury Hammel. Philadelphia became the first city to enter what is now a substantial BALLE network, thanks to the steering committee of the Sustainable Business Network of Philadelphia (SBN Philadelphia). Together with Michelle Long in Bellingham, Washington, they launched a movement that now embraces cities across the whole country.

This women-led movement is breaking away from the old-white-boy network paradigm that has dominated business since the Industrial Revolution. A study by the *Harvard Business Review* documented the proven superior management skills of women.[38] Looking at over 7,000 business leaders, the study ranked women above men on all levels of management in terms of overall effectiveness. This is a key element in the current paradigm shift and certainly essential to the success of BALLE.

While establishing my initial advisory business at Legg Mason, I needed a way to meet more like-minded investors. I was inspired to encourage SBN Philadelphia to develop the kind of "conversation circles" that built Philadelphia in the first place. The "Leather Apron Club" was a circle of craftsmen Benjamin Franklin met with regularly to solve local problems.[39] He would anonymously write up and circulate their proposals to influence public opinion. Without any political representation, these ideas instigated the first public library, voluntary fire department, sidewalks, and cobblestone streets.

Responding positively to my proposal, SBN Philadelphia started its own Circle of Entrepreneurs, a gathering for peer-to-peer support focused on one or two local businesses each meeting.

Members met each month for over ten years, sometimes in more than one location, fostering a sense of community and collaboration.

Meanwhile another group, Green Village Philadelphia, formed around the concept of creating a sustainable business center in the city where all kinds of green businesses could collaborate. We met for years, looking at one abandoned building or brown field after another—envisioning, arguing, and inspiring one another. More recently, two nonprofit incubators were merged to form the Good Company Group, soon to be the beneficiary of a prestigious Bloomberg Philanthropies Mayors Challenge grant.

INCUBATORS AND CROWDFUNDING

Such incubators are forming all over the country, like healthy economic cells. Some, like the Unreasonable Institute in Boulder, Colorado, have become international magnets for the best ideas in the world. Competitive RFPs gather hundreds of applicants for focused investment days where angels, foundations, and other impact investors gather to hear pitches. Meanwhile, local shared workspaces such as Impact Hubs are opening up for entrepreneurs to cohabitate, inspire, and collaborate. Most of these entrepreneurs are tech-oriented, but shared manufacturing spaces are also starting to take form.

Magically, one of the huge warehouses in which we tromped around years ago was acquired by Shift Capital, a New York–based investment firm, with help from iStartup's Janice Caillet. Perhaps our ideas lived on in the collective unconscious, later attracting those who could fulfill the vision! It is fun to imagine that huge warehouse carrying our dream like a sleeping giant.

Back then we could not imagine how to fund such a large undertaking, but now people can take advantage of online investing or crowdfunding, which has matured in the last few years.

Fundrise is a relatively new platform that allows local non-accredited investors to acquire funds through a direct public offering (DPO) by pooling their small investments together.[40] It is one of many such democratic initiatives to empower local investors. John Katovich of Cutting Edge Capital has developed his fundraising practice specifically around the DPO concept.[41]

Danae Ringelmann of Indiegogo initially wanted to help people launch plays and films.[42] When she realized that only 0.04 percent of new businesses receive venture backing and only 15 percent manage to secure loans, she built a platform wherein an individual can raise money from supporters in exchange for a small gift. So simple. User fees are increased if the goal is not reached, but unlike competitors such as Kickstarter, the money can still be accepted if you fall short of your stated goal. You can simply go for it and see what happens.

Such approaches are on track to raise billions of dollars from participants all over the globe, democratizing fundraising initiatives for valuable projects. When I saw her up on the stage at a gathering of the Social Venture Network, Ringelmann seemed so unlike the old archetypal capitalist. The times they are a-changin', thanks to the millennial generation, and Ringelmann is as straightforward as she is wildly successful! Her advice: Ask yourself, what bothers you the most? Why? What can be done about it? And who else cares? Then talk to others who care and imagine raising $100,000 to address the problem. Do it because you can. Millions of dollars are now being raised this way. Billions will be.

ALTERNATIVE BANKING

Others are democratizing the flow of capital outside the impersonal stock market and the tight bureaucracy of big banks. Connie Evans of the Association for Enterprise Opportunity has decades of experience finding social solutions and, like Danae, is most concerned about the lack of access to capital.[43] Because traditional banks are currently declining 8,000 loan applications every day, Evans is working with Muhammad Yunus of the Grameen Foundation to build micro-lending in this country.[44] She is also raising a $50 million American Dream Fund to lend up to $250,000 of unsecured debt with 20 percent turned around within forty-eight hours and four to six weeks if the borrower needs to receive advice along with the loan. The American Dream Fund expects to turn down only 7–10 percent of applicants and to work with the 70 percent who need advice.

On a global scale, as mentioned earlier, Kiva opened the door to altruistic lenders to make zero-interest loans to poor entrepreneurs in the majority (developing) world. Starting with loans at $25 a shot that link the lender to the entrepreneur through a Facebook-like directory, this vibrant initiative is also growing by the millions each month. The only limit is imagination—and the participation of intermediaries to ensure such loans get into the right hands. In order to break away from the current portfolio gridlock, new intermediaries are proposing to open the portals wide for web transactions directly between investors and investments. While creative initiatives are blossoming, regulatory scrutiny is expanding as well, so it is hard to say how this will play out.

SOCIAL NETWORKS FOR SOCIAL INVESTING

Our research team built WikiPositive as a wiki for socially positive investments. We currently list information on over 900 public companies with plans to expand with both public and private initiatives that benefit society. Currently the site is non-transactional and simply provides a starting point for research with links to deeper information. Over 700 companies on WikiPositive are linked to CSRHub, the largest aggregator of ratings data from around the globe. Users can use CSRHub to learn how a particular company rates compared to its peers in terms of environmental, social, and governance (ESG) ratings.

CSRHub.com has grown in leaps and bounds over the last five years. The user can drill down to see what data sources were used to rate each company, and reports can be purchased. The aim is to help companies improve their profiles, so the competition has become a race to the top, instead of a race to undermine, cut corners, or cheat to win.

The investment network Maximpact was built so that well-known managers can display private deals for impact investors to view and possibly connect over. Mission Markets and Gate Capital, on the other hand, are transactional platforms for impact investments. Mission Markets, along with its private offerings, has recognized the need for a broad database of global small-cap public companies that are not yet recognized by ESG reporting but clearly embrace socially beneficial missions. These and similar initiatives are springing up all over and, as they mature, will benefit from collaboration.

A small but powerful group of investors and nonprofit leaders, impact investors, and fund managers attend an annual retreat in Mexico to move this agenda forward. The Opportunity Collaboration, like the Clinton Global Initiative, is a way for thought leaders to discover how, through collaboration, to make a bigger positive difference.[45] Jonathan C. Lewis, a pioneer of socially responsible investing, founded this gathering in part to support the growth of MicroCredit Enterprises, an initiative to identify wealthy individuals willing to guarantee institutional loans for microcredit.[46] The clear focus of the retreat is on alleviating global poverty, but the broad range of discussions includes debates over key terms such as *sustainability* and *impact*.

The possibility of fiscal irresponsibility or mismanagement must always be considered. We can learn from the story of E+Co, which initially focused on bringing clean energy to developing countries. Impact investors were so successfully drawn to the company's concepts—such as providing electricity for Internet connectivity to remote parts of the globe—that the money came in too fast and managers were stretched too thin to monitor their global portfolios in a responsible manner. As a small but early investor, I represent the minority investors on Persistent Energy Partners, the advisory board overseeing the unwinding and focusing of E+Co. This is proceeding in an admirable fashion with far fewer losses than expected, but no one can afford to overlook the critical importance of cash flow and organizational management. The standards for impact investing must be just as high as for traditional investment practices.[47]

Terry Mollner, chair of StakeHolders Capital and one of the founders of the Calvert Foundation, argues that the next evolutionary step for humanity is for individuals and corporations to publicly prioritize the common good in their approach to *everything*, including, of course, investing. Many of the organizations and concepts mentioned in this chapter are in their infancy. I believe that one day there will be a new way for entrepreneurs to join with enlightened investors in order to produce common benefits. Here are a few suggestions:

- When forming socially beneficial funds, value all early dollars and late dollars invested equally, so there is no potential for the initiators to get robbed of control by "vulture capitalists."

- Value each entrepreneur's business and give them equity in the fund based on the valuation (e.g., a $100,000 valuation could give the company $100,000 in equity, just as though they put in capital).

- When designing funds, take into consideration the potential for shared resources and value adds, so that the companies in the fund benefit one another symbiotically.

- Recognize that some companies may fail, but their resources remain available to the rest—if any one company wins, they all win.

- Peer decisions can determine the need for new capital and where it would be most beneficial for the fund as a whole.

One thing is certain: Asset managers need innovative funds to reach this new economy—and they need to be guided well. They need a range of choices, packaged in understandable, accessible ways via trustworthy intermediaries. This is possible; it simply takes resolve, positive intentions, and a willingness to change. Hazel Henderson's "Green Economy" investment tracking has shown that the already-impressive shift to green investments is rapidly accelerating.[48] This is not simply altruism, but rather a practical response to world issues and a sound approach to long-term investing. It carries with it a sense of justice.

Benjamin Franklin's Virtues: Justice

"Wrong none by doing injuries, or omitting the benefits that are your duty."

Justice is so often confused with retribution and punishment. Franklin sees justice not as a Big Brother imposing penalties, but as a self-moderated virtue that is the duty of each and every person.

The greatest enemy of self-directed change is inertia. While experts are often needed to provide financial guidance, for justice to reign, we must not cede our moral obligations to "experts" who may not see justice as their responsibility. The "divest/invest" movement has awakened many investors to proactively take justice into their own hands, beginning with the fight against pollution caused by fossil-fuel extraction. This is only one of many important issues that investors can and do impact.

We must ourselves do no harm, but also depart from the status quo if something needs to be changed for the better. By supporting shortsighted corporations, we unconsciously do injury and omit our duty to support beneficial products and services. This is not so hard to change, because if we place our focus on justice, we will know when to act and when to stop.

CHAPTER 8:

REBIRTHING THE NATURAL STEP, INDUSTRY BY INDUSTRY

"Genius is the result of industry." —*Rudolf Steiner*

To invest in a coherent way, clients must let their advisors and consultants know what matters most to them. If you are socially conscious, discuss your passions and what you want and don't want to support. Your money is an expression of your intentions. Like smart shoppers who read the labels, investors who care about the planet are discriminating, choosing advisors who have access to and understanding of investments to match.

In *The Analysis of the Mind*, the philosopher Bertrand Russell notes that one can observe the most profound inner drama by watching how an individual deliberates, for example when shopping, hesitating, and trying to discern what products to take off the shelf and bring home. Each choice entails active moderation among memories, associations, soul needs, desires, and the priorities required by a limited budget. Producers and consumers both experience this same deep activity of discernment as they try to distinguish themselves in the market. What rules behavior, for better or for worse, is the unconscious or conscious preference that is "top of mind."

When a client is building a well-diversified investment portfolio, the same discernment is essential. Market watchers might shout to buy oil and tobacco while progressive investors have solar or fair-trade chocolate at "top of mind." We must moderate these influences to stay balanced and clear. Paul Herman helps us do so using this proven equation: Human + Impact = Profit, or HIP.[49]

Regardless of whether you are a "HIP" or "unhip" investor, the market can be divided into different industrial sectors of the world economy (for example, consumer products, commodities, electronics, energy, financials, technology, services, communications, utilities, manufacturing). The investor must discern, first of all, whether the profile reflects a monocultural investment strategy (too much tech in 2000 when the market was shouting TECH!) or forms an intelligent ecosystem that can survive tough times.

When considering each sector, a conscious or HIP investor should reflect upon what is most important in each aspect of the world's economies. What might be "top of mind" when choosing consumer staples or consumer discretionary stocks, energy/utilities, electronics/telecom, healthcare, financials, and so on? What guiding quality is valued most when deciding to invest? The individual investor's discretion will become the virtue of markets.

Most investors lack even a framework for creating such guidelines. If we value only *more money*, we let the fox into the henhouse and all human values will be mauled. Recently, an old tune caught my attention with these catchy words: "Who broke the lock? Who broke the lock on the hen house door? Who broke the lock? I don't know . . . I'm a-gonna find out before I go . . ." So who snuck into the hen house, where eggs are laid and value is produced? Isn't that a question for our financial world?

If we are only interested in generating more money, then we are the ones who broke the lock. For example, investing in multinational agricultural corporations intent on destroying local organic markets may seem smart if pure profit is the goal. On the other hand, helping end industrial agriculture is the first step towards shaping a better world. But for such an action to make sense, we need a new "lock." That is, we need an investor movement with strong principles to guide decisions both locally and globally.

If we only dream about becoming the richest or most powerful person, business, or nation, the "chickens" will run away or get mauled. Fortunately, there are many moral and ethical frameworks that can protect us from mismanaging our resources. One good example is the Natural Step approach.[50]

Swedish researchers developed the Natural Step decision tree to help counter the outrageous fact that, global warming aside, most cancers are environmentally caused and avoidable.[51] If we could only persuade businesses to consider the Natural Step approach before making decisions, these environmental cancers might go away. After producing volumes of research, the researchers narrowed their thesis down to four simple steps. Their website provides the following chart breaking down certain systemic problems into four steps:

THE FOUR SYSTEM CONDITIONS	REWORDED AS THE FOUR SUSTAINABILITY PRINCIPLES
In a sustainable society, nature is not subject to *systematically increasing*:	To become a sustainable society, we must eliminate our contributions to:
(1) Concentrations of substances extracted from the earth's crust,	(1) The *systematic increase* of concentrations of substances extracted from the earth's crust (for example, heavy metals and fossil fuels);
(2) Concentrations of substances produced by society,	(2) The *systematic increase* of concentrations of substances produced by society (for example, plastics, dioxins, PCBs, and DDT);
(3) Degradation by physical means,	(3) The *systematic* physical degradation of nature and natural processes (for example, overharvesting forests, destroying habitat, and overfishing); and
(4) And, in that society, people are not subject to conditions that *systemically* undermine their capacity to meet their needs.	(4) Conditions that *systematically* undermine people's capacity to meet their basic human needs (for example, unsafe working conditions and not enough pay to live on).

Simplifying these four principles, the original elevator pitch was: avoid extraction, avoid chemical compounds that don't occur in nature, avoid the degradation of nature, and take care of human needs.

Our research has modified these principles. Instead of focusing on negative screening or avoidance, we choose to focus on positive solutions for investment. Our research team prioritizes investment options like so:

1. First take care of human needs *by investing in essential products and services.* In doing so:

2. Avoid extracting substances from below the earth's crust, *and value companies that recycle, reduce, and reuse;*

3. Avoid developing and using chemical compounds that do not occur in nature, *focusing rather on natural solutions and products;* and

4. Avoid the degradation of nature and the exploitation of people and planet, *while finding ways to enhance life in the biosphere.*

These guidelines are like a good lock. No one is forced to comply with them, but the hens will sleep peacefully if the principles behind them prevail. What is stopping us?

Common sense dictates that we should invest in products and services that meet human needs. The problem is that businesses have forgotten that their main purpose is to take care of human needs! As consumers and investors, we can support products and services that actually matter. Would portfolios suffer? Not if consumers and producers unite as a movement to insist on best practices.

By expanding from the congested "Wall Street" universe of

stocks, one can enter much broader global public and private markets, as well as lend within local economies. In a world where human values matter, good companies will be highly valued and bad ones shunned. This is like letting the hens out to range on fresh ground by day and wisely locking the door at night. In the meantime, ethical investors can save a ton of time by analyzing only companies they believe to be inherently beneficial.

Investors are more satisfied once they can synthesize their values with their investments. Farsighted analysts understand that metrics are most valuable in the context of a meaningful matrix. Rather than analyzing *any* prospective investment based on a good financial record, research would then begin with the primary "natural step": taking care of human needs. In other words, first look at the whole and make a heart-centered decision about what the world needs now. Then do the research, seeking products and services to meet those needs. That is the matrix for the new economics going forward.

Max Neef, the Nobel laureate in economics, created a new framework for understanding human needs (see below) that does not prioritize needs in the form of a hierarchical pyramid. To Neef, all needs are equally important, whether considering a physical need (the need for food, clothing, and shelter), an emotional need (the need for community and being loved), or a spiritual need (the need to be creative and free as an individual).

Fundamental Human Needs	Being (qualities)	Having (things)	Doing (actions)	Interacting (settings)
subsistence	physical and mental health	food, shelter, work	feed, clothe, rest, work	living environment, social setting
protection	care, adaptability, autonomy	social security, health systems, work	cooperate, plan, take care of, help	social environment, dwelling
affection	respect, sense of humor, generosity, sensuality	friendships, family, relationships with nature	share, take care of, make love, express emotions	privacy, intimate spaces of togetherness
understanding	critical capacity, curiosity, intuition	literature, teachers, educational policies	analyze, study, meditate, investigate	schools, families, universities, communities
participation	receptiveness, dedication, sense of humor	responsibilities, duties, work, rights	cooperate, dissent, express opinions	associations, parties, churches, neighborhoods
leisure	imagination, tranquility, spontaneity	games, parties, peace of mind	day-dream, remember, relax, have fun	landscapes, intimate spaces, places to be alone
creation	imagination, boldness, inventiveness, curiosity	abilities, skills, work techniques	invent, build, design, work, compose, interpret	spaces for expression, workshops, audiences
identity	sense of belonging, self-esteem, consistency	language, religions, work, customs, values, norms	get to know oneself, grow, commit oneself	places one belongs to, everyday settings
freedom	autonomy, passion, self-esteem, open-mindedness	equal rights	dissent, choose, run risks, develop awareness	anywhere

In working with this new framework, I like to consider the needs categories in three groups: first, *subsistence, protection,* and *leisure* are most related to physical needs (leisure implies the need to rest, recuperate and rejuvenate); second, *affection, understanding,* and *participation* are related to emotional needs; while *creation, identity,* and *freedom* are related to spiritual needs, such as the need for self-expression and realization.

The simplest way for the investor or analyst to focus on meeting human needs is to ask, "What real human need can this industry provide for?" For example, when considering what is most needed for consumer staples, the word *nourishment* comes to mind. The need for nourishment can likewise be understood in three ways. On the physical level, one is nourished not only by healthful food but also by the safety and wholesomeness of one's surroundings. In the emotional realm, nourishment comes from knowing local growers and how they care for land and animals. ("Fair trade" certified products also give a feeling of connection and understanding of where food comes from.) Spiritually, nutritive forces sustain the quality of our thinking and the strength of our will to make a difference as free and ethical individuals.

The environmentalist Paul Hawken once shared with me that reading Steiner's *Agriculture Course* inspired him to found Erewhon, the first large-scale distributor of organic and biodynamic food in the United States. Hawken was inspired by Steiner's concept that the quality of our food influences the way we think and increases our capacity to understand. Hawken put this idea "top of mind" and put his resources immediately into action. Since the 1970s, "we are what we eat" has become an accepted cultural maxim, sparking the local, organic, and "slow food" renaissance.

For retail investors in public markets, identifying organic and fair-trade companies is still difficult. In the meantime, this investment category can be satisfied in other ways such as shopping at farmers markets or lending funds to local farmers through Slow Money. Institutional and "ultra-high net worth" investors are seeking ways to restore farmland through regenerative practices and improve food production using advanced storage and processing systems. Eventually, it all leads to real nourishment.

The choices for investment in each industry class can go through the same kind of prioritization process, placing what is needed most at "top of mind." The Resources section in the back of this book contains a working list with guiding thoughts for each industry. Researchers and serious impact investors can use this to study and evolve on their own.

At this time, the Divest-Invest Movement is focusing on the fossil-fuel industry and the energy and utility sectors. The Natural Step decision tree would avoid extraction, choosing natural and renewable sources of energy instead.

Bill McKibben's global awareness campaign, 350.org, centers on the fact that carbon in the atmosphere has exceeded 350 parts per million.[52] Once this tipping point is reached and balance is disrupted, previously unnatural occurrences—like excessive cold or heat, deluge, or drought—become common. It will take a lot of butterflies to turn this around. In the meantime, renewable energy stocks have been extremely volatile. Thanks to the flood of cheap solar panels from China and the 2012 "Solyndra scandal" regarding solar company subsidizations, many renewable-energy stocks have cratered and then rebounded in recent years. Only with an evolving consciousness and subsequent investor and consumer demand will renewable energy maintain its proper valuation in this critical moment of history. To quote from 350.org:

> Getting (back) to 350 means developing a thousand different solutions—all of which will become much easier if we have a global treaty grounded in the latest science and built around the principles of equity and justice. To get this kind of treaty, we need a movement of people who care enough about our shared global future to get involved and make their voices heard.[53]

A few immediate and efficient ways to invest in cutting energy cost include improving insulation and energy monitoring techniques in new structures while intelligently retrofitting old buildings. This was recently done to the Empire State Building by Jonathan Rose, who manages Rose Smart Growth Fund, one of only three "green" real estate funds I am aware of at this time.[54] 5Stone Capital Partners has recently begun developing properties as well, and Amero Global Investors in Atlanta is seeking operating capital.[55,56] With any luck, energy based on solar, wind, fuel cell, tides, and algae will regain their rightful valuations, and we will proudly dive below 350 and breathe normally again. For now, we must fight to see this happen.

The time is ripe to divest from fossil fuels, which can be done sanely and with full fiduciary responsibility. Why not discuss the possibility? Divestment is simply the right and prudent decision. Unless things change dramatically, financial experts on the boards of endowments may one day look down on the earth's smoldering remains and comfort themselves by asserting that at least they did their "fiduciary duty" by putting profits first!

Students at Swarthmore College, in protest of fossil fuel–linked investments, took over and shut down a meeting on the college endowment. On May 9, 2013, the Swarthmore *Daily Gazette* published an article about Chris Niemczewski, an "expert" from the investment committee, who claimed that divestment would cost the endowment over $200 million over ten years. Niemczewski's argument was full of stretched truths and hidden assumptions; for example, he ignored the possibility that reduced costs of renewable alternatives could dramatically change the valuation of oil. In response to such a loose, poorly conceived argument, one could offer this quick, "back of an envelope" response:

1. Since 80 percent of oil reserves can never be burned as fossil fuels (if continued life on the planet is considered important), the value of oil stocks cannot reflect those reserves as an asset.

2. In fact oil stocks can be considered a liability since the continued depletion of our atmosphere (now at 400 ppm!) will likely result in class action lawsuits.

3. Projected over time, the holding of oil-related stocks, now, say, 5 percent of the endowment's portfolio overvalued by at least 80 percent means a likely loss of 4 percent of the value of the portfolio per year for the next ten years.

4. Based on similar guesswork, these dirty investments could cost the university as much as $600 million!

Many studies show that, contrary to popular belief, socially responsible criteria and negative screening cannot be shown statistically to have an impact on performance. Researchers in general cannot say whether negative screening has any reliable financial impact, positive or negative, because, on average, all managers underperform their benchmarks by the amount they charge in fees.

Even though no one *seems* to be listening, and though one might not hear what is being said through the cheers and chants, student protestors *are* getting attention. Endowments and financial institutions across the country are divesting or are considering doing so, buying fossil-free funds and making their own measured choices instead. According to *Greenbiz*, Norway's Storebrand, which holds more than $30 billion in assets, has excluded thirteen coal and six tar sands companies from all investments "to reduce Storebrand's exposure to fossil fuels and to secure long-term, stable returns for our clients."[57] Similarly, in December 2014 Germany's largest utility, Eon, began spinning off its fossil fuel–fired plants to concentrate on renewable energy.[58] In 2014, Paul Herman compiled an important white paper on the economics of divestment with an appendix listing a few leading fossil-free funds.[59]

We are beyond the neutral point. Even if one could argue that we had nothing to do with this dramatic weather, we certainly can help mitigate its effects by investing in a world that is more likely to last.

Benjamin Franklin's Virtues: Cleanliness

"Tolerate no uncleanliness in body, cloaths, or habitation."

Keeping clean was not easy in Ben Franklin's day, and one needed to make cleanliness a priority to stay healthy. Franklin was known to believe in fresh air, and he cooled off and aired his bed by keeping his windows open through the night. In the financial world, if asset owners and their advisors would clean up their portfolios, a healthier planet would result. Only investing in beneficial products and services is an important start.

Like forgotten cobwebs, the small print of many offerings needs to be cleaned up. I will always be grateful to a mentor who pointed out to me the importance of reading the fine print in bond funds prior to the crash of 2008. Many funds even today are highly leveraged, which means that much of the money invested in the fund is borrowed. If the fund value goes down too much and the loans are called, the original investors will suffer from accelerated losses. This seems intolerably "unclean" to me. Nowadays, it is essential to scrub all offerings or legal documents and make sure there are no hidden cobwebs.

CHAPTER 9:

FROM 5% TO 100%, EVERY INVESTMENT HAS IMPACT

*"No problem can be solved from the same level of
consciousness that created it." —Albert Einstein*

I first met Jay Coen Gilbert, founder of B Lab, the nonprofit behind the B- Corporation concept, at one of his Spirit in Business meetings.[60] Afterwards, I invited the group to one of my Circle of Entrepreneurs meetings, and Jay showed up. He liked the way we had created something out of nothing, a talent he certainly displayed by founding AND1, a successful basketball shoe and apparel company, and continues to show as B Lab blossoms globally. The Circle was attracting such an enthusiastic group of entrepreneurs that it had begun to feel like a truly caring community.

Jay and I talked at length about Paul Newman's amazing model, Newman's Own, which donates 100 percent of profits to charity. Inspired by Gandhi's purported statement that "we must *be* the change we seek in the world," and the help of Untours founder Hal Taussig, the idea for B-Corporations was born.

The original idea was to create a fund by investing only in what we called "Newman Ventures," companies that donate 100 percent of profits to charity. Over time, that idea morphed into a for-profit fund of companies that are committed to meeting high standards of social and environmental performance, transparency, and legal accountability. When taken public, these companies would inoculate the "market" with a positive antidote against the Wall Street culture of greed. In other words, trading for-benefit companies on the public market could demonstrate that these standards would be highly valued by investors in terms of stock price, despite costs involved in considering employees, customers and the environment.

Today, B Lab has certified over 900 companies as having met these standards. Now this community of businesses is storming the statehouses. One by one, states are passing laws to create a new corporate structure that allows companies to be publicly accountable for their impacts on society, not just shareholders. Technically, these new entities are called "Benefit Corporations."

According to Jay in a recent email exchange, "B-Corps try to avoid 'green-washing' by having their social and environmental performance assessed and verified by an independent nonprofit organization (B Lab), by making that verified performance transparent and available on bcorporation.net, and by amending their legal documents to give shareholders new rights to hold management accountable to achieve social, not just financial, objectives."

All generalized rating systems, whether done internally or externally, are by nature imperfect because each endeavor is more or less unique. The weighting of factors to rate the benefit of corporations may not be entirely fair. Ideally, the actual benefit of investments made by financial institutions should be weighted above 90 percent.

IMPACT FUNDS AND BENEFIT CORPORATIONS

Now B Lab has also taken up the external rating of "impact funds" via B Analytics, a data platform for measuring, benchmarking, and reporting on impact, developed primarily by Beth Richardson. In a parallel initiative, Jed Emerson leads a group to choose the annual "Impact50" list of their favorite impact funds for each year, with hundreds vying for inclusion. The winners show a wide range of style and substance, from low financial return and high social or environmental return, to higher financial return and perhaps less social relevance.[61]

Over time, standards will continue to rise until investors can choose from a plethora of funds that meet the sustainable financial goals of a pension fund while providing cleaner air, water, soil, access, security, health, wellness, empowerment, and even inspiration. The consequences of benefit corporations are potentially game changing. Increasingly freed from purely monetary considerations, executives will be encouraged to make important beneficial decisions for the common good. Their companies' valuation, in the transformed marketplace, will increasingly include external rates of return—the degree to which they add measurable value to all external stakeholders, and ultimately the common wealth of the planet.

Stuart Williams of Endobility argues that the way we think about wealth creation should expand to include employees, communities, the environment, supply chains, and financial investors.[62] His Alabaster Jar Foundation lists specific goals related to this paradigm shift: 12,000 global companies need to be restructured as benefit corporations, and 50 percent of new companies in the future need to register as such. These are achievable goals. The challenge is one of leadership and communication: inspiring the change and arguing for the mutual benefits of this approach.

A few years ago, I was privileged to hear Jeffrey Hollander, founder of Seventh Generation, speak at a Social Venture Network meeting about CEO leadership. His words should be repeated again and again until the culture of business is healed: "Whenever a CEO says they can't do something that is good because they might be sued, they are simply exposing their own lack of courage and conviction."

To lead an organization takes inner fire. If inspired by greed, the fire will burn out quickly. If inspired by a desire to do good, the fire will last and spread to keep warm other employees, investors, and community stakeholders. Greed isolates and creates a chilly work environment, while altruism leads to collaborative, lasting relationships.

The nonprofit group Trust Across America has been tracking the trustworthiness of large corporations for over a decade.[63] Not surprisingly, the most "trustworthy" of these corporations, as a group, have outperformed peer corporations in long-term success. Investments in these companies have been rewarded. Creating for-benefit business cultures that inspire trust takes passion and deeper reasons for being in business altogether. But "green-washing" is rampant, and checks and balances are needed to ensure that venture leaders are genuine.

CORPORATIONS, GOVERNMENT, AND ETHICS

One way to define the "one percent" decried by Occupy Wall Street is "corporate management, on the C-level": CEOs, COOs, CIOs—in other words, the chiefs. In a socialistic society, the chiefs of industry may in fact be heads of government. (Vladimir Putin is often referred to as an oligarch and Europe's richest man.) In a capitalistic society, they may have such influence in governments that they might as well be running them. We need to agree on new standards for the rest of the "chiefs"—starting with the Commander-in-Chief, our president.

Herein lies a major problem. The scale and complexity of today's world requires massive control of the means of production, natural resources, and man-made infrastructures. Economic considerations are mixed into government mandates, whether the government is democratically elected or not. As President Bill Clinton reminded himself daily, "It's the economy, stupid!" Instead of justice or human rights, the true domain of government, he felt it was his job as a politician to manage the economy, and so it took priority.

If we have any hope for a better world, the chiefs must prioritize the common good above profit. In other words, "C-level" executives should remain on that level only if their leadership is in the best interests of society. This is a matter of good governance, a matter for corporate boards. It is also a matter of good education. Empathy is a natural human capacity, but it certainly can be unlearned—especially when bad behavior is rewarded.

Ethics must be taught as a framework for decision-making, even if only in the mind and individual will of the managers in charge. Across the country, from Bainbridge Island in Washington State to Marlboro, Vermont, sustainable MBA programs are springing up to guide the new business leaders. (See appendix for a list.) Even Harvard MBAs agree to an oath, not unlike the Hippocratic oath taken by medical doctors to first do no harm.

THE HARVARD MBA OATH

As a business leader, I recognize my role in society.

- My purpose is to lead people and manage resources to create value that no single individual can create alone.

- My decisions affect the well-being of individuals inside and outside my enterprise, today and tomorrow.

Therefore, I promise that:

- I will manage my enterprise with loyalty and care, and will not advance my personal interests at the expense of my enterprise or society.

- I will understand and uphold, in letter and spirit, the

laws and contracts governing my conduct and that of my enterprise.

• I will refrain from corruption, unfair competition, or business practices harmful to society.

• I will protect the human rights and dignity of all people affected by my enterprise, and I will oppose discrimination and exploitation.

• I will protect the right of future generations to advance their standard of living and enjoy a healthy planet.

• I will report the performance and risks of my enterprise accurately and honestly.

• I will invest in developing myself and others, helping the management profession continue to advance and create sustainable and inclusive prosperity.

In exercising my professional duties according to these principles, I recognize that my behavior must set an example of integrity, eliciting trust and esteem from those I serve. I will remain accountable to my peers and to society for my actions and for upholding these standards.

This oath I make freely, and upon my honor.

Finally, it is time to unblur the lines between government, business, and education. If the sole mandate of good government is to protect human rights and the ideal of equality and justice for all, it cannot allow the influence of industrial chiefs to favor their economic interests.

CEOs educated to be in touch with their own goodwill would not seek such leverage. This is what has driven long-term thinkers at Ashoka, Bill Drayton's network of social entrepreneurs, to think about new ways of bringing empathy back into our culture. They describe it this way: "Ashoka's Empathy Initiative is a collaborative platform for social entrepreneurs and others who share this vision of a world where every child masters empathy." Drayton aims to foster a society "in which empathy learning is as fundamental as reading and math."[64]

Once again, a positive social future requires:

1. An education system that encourages empathy and ethical individualism;

2. A government that focuses primarily on human rights and justice for all, leaving the business chiefs out of it; and

3. Corporate self-governance that mandates leadership to maximize real profit, that is, profit as a boon to society as realized through products and services that benefit the environment and the local and global community.

These three goals provide a "rising global C-level" to meet the needs and overcome the fears and dangers of our time.

As we spend more time looking for honorable companies, the "best of the worst" approach to investing must be rejected. Many businesses, such as a certain famous oil company with the sun logo, are just "green-washing" themselves to flatter our wishes for a better world. As the famously imperfect architect and visionary, William McDonough, coauthor of *Cradle to Cradle*, likes to say, "I am tired of less bad!" For example, measuring the reduction in carbon footprints is, of course, crucial, and is already being done more and more. We need to measure what matters, and carbon markets increase the focus on pollution for the benefit of all. However, more resources must be directed to solutions that replace fossil based products or directly reduce the carbon in the atmosphere. One way to accelerate the search for solutions is to link international experts and investors with positive enterprises. Heather White is in a good position to help this happen. The founder of Verité and New Standards, she has uncovered labor issues in sixty countries over the last fifteen years by working with an extraordinary network of researchers all over the world.[65] The challenge is how to use valuable human resources, such as Heather's group of personally vetted researchers, to help uncover and perform due diligence on this promising new wave of benefit corporations.

These resources could be used to track benefits and customize ratings for individual interest groups, family offices, foundations, and other social enterprises. This has been Sarah Olsen's approach at Social Venture Technology for over a decade, but more such groups are needed.[66] Standardization of ratings is necessary, but we must be able to recognize and track specific and unique outcomes as well.

In farming, I learned to focus resources on fostering the best land and healthiest animals first, rather than spending too much time and effort on the least fruitful fields and weakest animals. In time an inherently strong ecosystem develops. Once projects become self-supporting, more time and energy can be spent rejuvenating the less strong. By finding, fostering, and funding positive initiatives, our goal as fund managers is to focus on the best innovations in the world.

WikiPositive is designed to allow a global open-source network, a "smart mob" of researchers, to find these innovations. In future, WikiPositive may provide a searchable list of experts available for due diligence on a one-time or long-term basis. Like the coders behind Linux, these experts may contribute to this new economic paradigm simply to see the world benefit from their work. If paid, the cost would be small compared to the cost of a fulltime in-house staff. This grand vision requires a great deal of collaboration on all sides. But once investors are given the tools to find the best solutions to today's problems and investment offerings that make a difference, they will be in a better position to help the planet.

Benjamin Franklin's Virtues: Chastity

"Rarely use venery but for health or offspring, never to dullness, weakness, or to the injury of your own or another's peace or reputation."

The male hormone testosterone has become a drug of choice for Wall Street traders, encouraging them to jump into the fray and make bolder, riskier decisions, to stand out from the crowd and push themselves ahead. The relationship between sexuality and money is blatantly obvious, given the size of the sex industry and the use of sexual imagery in advertising.

Franklin's advice easily works as a guide to those addicted to the stimulation of "the market" or the allure of credit cards. If our attitude to money is chastened, we can enjoy money without "injury of [our] own or another's peace or reputation."

PART III:

WHAT WILL INSPIRE US?

CHAPTER 10:

SUSTAINABLE AGRICULTURE, SYSTEMS THINKING, AND INVESTING

"We can move from shallow efficiency to deep effectiveness."
—Katherine Collins in The Nature of Investing

We live in a time of crisis. Despite climbing to new heights, the health of the financial markets is uncertain at best; some local and national governments cannot sell enough bonds to secure funds for basic operations, not to mention infrastructure, and at least 10 percent of able workers in well-to-do nations are unable to earn a living. Meanwhile, the environment is under stress. Global *weirding*, if not global warming, is happening, with droughts in one hemisphere, floods in another, cold in places that are usually hot, and hot where it's usually cold.

Often ignored is the unprecedented response by NGOs around the world to resolve environmental problems and develop a sustainable world design. Likewise, the possibility of a parallel financial crisis demands a new approach to money and investment. One way out is offered by the environmentalist and entrepreneur Paul Hawken in his book *Blessed Unrest*.[67] Hawken reckons that somewhere between one and two million organizations have self-selected to make a positive difference since the beginning of the millennium.

Hawken also identifies the greatest challenge of our time: Only a small percentage of educated and wealthy people control the commercial world, and they have invested primarily in a world that is not ecologically sustainable, politically just, or spiritually free. This includes investors in 401(k) and pension plans, as well as wealthy families, foundations, and sovereign wealth plans. It includes people who consider themselves socially responsible but naïve in the realm of money. Trillions of dollars/euros/renminbi/yen are being invested to create a world that few would choose to live in!

This approach is not unlike the farmer who decides to bulldoze all his land for the sake of one cash crop, forgetting to leave the topsoil required for it to grow. In the guise of financial planners, advisors, and brokers, expert salesmen have convinced us that investing outside the very liquid Wall Street market is too unprofitable or risky, leading investors to ignore long-term sustainability and stick with the illusion of security in the status quo. Many do not know what they are investing in, like homeowners who use Agent Orange to kill dandelions and allow their children to play on toxic turf. We must remember the Chinese proverb that states, "The frog does not drink up the pond in which it lives." Clearly, some common-sense wisdom from sustainable agriculture could help bring us back on course.

LIGHT REINS

In my twenties, I wanted to learn how to farm with horses. I joined a community in order to apprentice with an experienced farmer and learn how an intentional community successfully manages money. I worked with a beautiful pair of Morgan/Percheron crosses, Bootch and Nellie. Together we cultivated three to five acres of vegetables. The work was fast and wonderfully silent, and our footprint created little or no compaction of the subsoil (as tractors tend to do), keeping it friable for roots to penetrate deeply. But I had to stay awake on the reins. Bootch might try to grab a greedy mouthful of something off to the side, or Nellie might pull toward the security of the barn. With a light hand on the reins, both horses tended to stay on course, keeping up their exquisite gliding momentum.

Investors should always remember that fear might pull one toward the safety of cash, while greed can entice one to take too much risk. Studies have shown that most long-term investors do not do as well as the mutual funds they own because they tend to buy into funds that are doing well, greedily expecting more growth, just when they are about to trend back to a more reasonable valuation (called "buying high"). Then when the stock price is undervalued, the investors sell after a downturn, fearfully expecting the worst to come, when in fact the fund was just about to recover (called "selling low").

It is normal to want to buy a certain stock when hearing how well others have done with it, but this may actually herald the end of a trend and indicate that it's time to sell. Similarly, when an investor seems to be losing money, what seems like a good time to sell might actually be the best time to buy.

Advisors usually try to persuade clients to "stay the course," which, in general, is better than being driven by emotion. In fact, good managers can successfully read the trends and carefully trim overvalued positions while adding to positions that are undervalued. This sophisticated work must be done objectively and proactively, rather than reactively. "Light reins" is the key.

WE ARE WHAT WE EAT

More and more, the lessons learned from farming seem relevant to resolving the disconnection between individuals with healthy dreams and their responsibility to protect their own resources. In fact, everything I needed to know to become a good steward of money I learned as a farmer in my twenties and early thirties.

The future depends on us reconnecting with the wisdom inherent in sustainable agriculture. This agricultural orientation includes the concurrent benefit of better nutrition, which may lead to freer thinking. After all, the phrase "we are what we eat" really means that *we are what we think we are*, because we choose how we eat. We reinforce our particular way of being by *eating what we want*. This reciprocal relationship is a closed cycle unless we can step out of our routine and take a look. The choice of food itself reflects our perspective. If we are inclined to think less, we might prefer comfort foods that keep us heavy, for example, while if we are spiritually motivated, we might be less likely to eat meat. This should not be taken dogmatically, as each person is unique.

The point is simply that thinking and eating are related, and together they affect who we become. Who we are, or aspire to be, determines whether or not we will invest in a conscious and caring way. We are all connected in this world economy, and, like it or not, no one else seems to be in charge. We need to love the whole thing and be good stewards of "Spaceship Earth," as Buckminster Fuller used to call it.

Experienced farmers often know their whole farms intimately, aware of every nook and cranny, and while seeing the entire place as a living organism. At Emerson College, I apprenticed with an old Swiss farmer who sensed things each day out of her natural awareness of the whole. She was suspicious of metrics and forbade me to count the cattle when we went to check them at their hillside pasture high above the barns. "If you have to count, you are not using your sense of the whole herd!" Had there been unrest in a far corner of the field while I was busy counting, I might not have noticed that the fence was broken and cattle had wandered to the other side.

Metrics are of limited usefulness for evaluating impact unless researchers step back to see the entire picture. Without this perspective, they will continue measuring how much "less bad" things are instead of addressing the deeper underlying problems.

DEEP DIGGING

Investors must also step back and consider all of their resources in order to determine the relationships between their various investments. Ideally, the blend will provide just the right combination of risk/return and social/environmental impact over an appropriate timeframe. This kind of thinking is natural to experienced gardeners, who can sense what plants go well together. They will surround carrots with onions, tomatoes with marigolds, and so on. Some of the reasons for these actions are logical and measurable—fewer insect pests from the marigolds and increased flavor for the carrots—but good gardeners don't need to measure. They can see and taste the difference.

It is possible to develop the common sense needed to judge whether a product or service is beneficial. Investments can be conceptualized as a manifold variety of plantings at different stages of maturity, each plant benefiting the common good in its own way, all synergistically supporting one another. As crops are rotated to benefit the soil, so some investments are harvested and others planted in an ecological procession. In a living system, the proportions of the ingredients change much like seasonal recipes.

With investing, as in healthy home gardening, much "deep digging" is needed before planting. The biodynamic/French Intensive concept of double digging taught me the importance of preparing the ground well. To make a raised bed—providing more air, more light, better water retention, and deeper roots—one starts by:

1. Digging out chunks a spade's length deep across the first row of the bed and setting the chunks neatly aside in a wheelbarrow without disturbing the topsoil.

2. Moving the second row up to where the first had been and continuing row by row until the entire bed has been

worked. The chunks of soil move forward by rows like musical chairs, and the chunks from the first row are taken out of the wheelbarrow and become the last row.

3. Before each row moves forward, it is important to dig down deep into the subsoil, rocking the spade back and forth to loosen and lift it for aeration and to invite the entry of deep roots. When all the rows are aerated below and moved, just add compost on top and watch the results!

Similarly, dig as deep as possible before making your investment. Get to know the management team and the business model and understand their true goals. A conscious investor cannot just rake the surface with a shallow understanding and hope to find good soil below. Deeper questions must be asked: Is the product or service beneficial and relevant? Is the business model progressive? Are they committed to fair wages and benefits, with ergonomic and safe systems of production? Do communities directly benefit or pay an unreasonable price for hosting them? Are the managers farsighted and sufficiently committed to benefit all stakeholders, not just themselves and other insiders?

All of this due diligence will help the investor prosper and benefit society and the planet at the same time. *Money is an expression of our highest intention*, even if that intention is only to want more money. These days, money is considered the goal for most endeavors. Money wants more money, an illusory cycle that only ends in dissatisfaction or worse. Plants grown without topsoil are needy in the same way.

THE LOVE OF MONEY

I believed for years the often-misquoted phrase from the Epistle to Timothy in the New Testament, "Money is the root of all evil." The correct phrase is "The love of money is the root of all evil." Money itself does not cause the trouble! It is the love—the intention—that is misplaced, wreaking havoc on our entire world culture. Money can serve as a tool to cultivate our world and help us reap harvests worthy of our humanity. Simply chasing after money distracts us from achieving truly important goals, which money can't buy.

The belief that we are here to make money has become a cultural norm that drives education, politics, and, of course, finance. Instead, we must turn Clinton's campaign slogan on its head: If we believe the economy is everything, then we are stupid. Our intentions live in the culture, which determines how we value things; the economy only follows suit. Agriculture, the way we relate to the land and feed ourselves, is at the root of it all! Agribusiness tries to take the culture out of it.

Investing, like farming, is both an art and a science, and intuition can be a significant aid to serious investors who have the capacity to read economic trends. Qualitative insight is needed to assess the value of large-scale infrastructure decisions, right down to the detailed impact of products and services on individual lives.

The world economy has an unhealthy distribution system and could use a new model. Money is trapped in the hands of big banks and hoarders who live off the income and never touch the principal; the idle money is either useless or damaging to society, depending on how it is invested. Nature could, perhaps, serve as inspiration. Trees demonstrate a beautiful distribution of form, from their massive trunks to the tiniest stems and root hairs. Portfolios should be designed using a systemic awareness of both the macro-economy and the details that affect individual workers and consumers.

THE FRACTAL MODEL

Nowadays, evolutionary researchers like Sally Goerner, author of *After the Clockwork Universe*, would call these examples of fractals: beautiful systems that replicate patterns, with a relationship between the constraints of efficient order and the diversity and freedom of flow. Think rivers, trees, lightning, and snowflakes. Healthy, resilient patterns are identifiable throughout nature, but are largely missing, crude, or imbalanced in our financial systems. Researching the social impact of investments is expensive, and investing big money in big projects is often easier when in fact that money could be more effectively spent a little at a time.

The fractal model provides a wonderful image for the circulation of money and distribution of values—whether considering the whole economy or a single organization, from the mission statement right down to individual interactions.

What is particularly extraordinary in trees is that the system, a big trunk with smaller and smaller branches both above and below the surface, only appears to be hierarchical. Consider how the hairs of the roots engage with multitudes of microorganisms that feed the tree, while the magic of photosynthesis takes place in the finest cells of the leaves. The trunk appears quite passive, providing infrastructure but not life. Companies that begin with healthy interactions on the management level provide good roots, while people in the field who carry out the same values with genuine integrity are leaves, taking in the sunshine of human interaction.

Elsie Maio of SoulBranding has studied the economic merit of soulful human values for over a decade, starting with a study she conducted at IBM in the 1990s. Her conclusions are clear: when the integrity of the whole is reflected in the details, value is generated beyond the norm. In the new money paradigm, corporations and financial systems will follow the wisdom of fractals and trees, wherein the best designs of nature effectively and efficiently carry the flow from the core to the periphery. Everything in our world economy has the potential to replicate this beautiful efficiency, from massive production down to design and implementation. Take healthcare, for example. With all the public debate about healthcare, it is easy to forget that, at its core, healthcare is *not* about big business; it is about the people on the periphery who are suffering. The details are in the look, the bedside manner, the touch, and the relationship. Systems that personalize care are most rewarding as they deliver the most healthful results.

Goerner tries to translate network science based on living systems into practical economic remedies, including for healthcare. Fractals demonstrate the dynamic between the efficient core of any system and the resilience, freedom, and diversity found in the periphery. Here are some of her thoughts in relation to money:

Fractal Civilization and Sustainable Prosperity

Sally Goerner

Most people see fractals as curious images, but their real message is that *everything* in the cosmos—including living, nonliving, and supra-living organizations such as economies—are part of a breathtakingly intricate design that we are only now beginning to understand scientifically. Naturally, rediscovering this cosmic design confirms a long list of spiritual and philosophical insights, but understanding how these designs work in real-world systems has also led to a remarkably practical explanation of how to build durably vibrant human networks as well. The surprising result is a commonsense explanation of why moral sentiments such as fairness, community, and integrity are essential to building vibrant economic networks capable of producing sustainable prosperity and well-being for all.

The basic lesson of fractal networks is that economic health is a function of *human networks*, and that the way to create prosperity for all is to apply nature's rules for creating durably vibrant networks to economies. Since circulation and flow are critical to vitality, the key image is of a healthy metabolism. Here, for example, money is like blood, a means of moving resources and catalyzing crucial processes, not an end in itself.

Rule #1: *Robust cross-scale circulation is crucial to everyone's health.*

Because the butcher, the baker, and the candlestick-maker all depend upon having a healthy and *complete economic circuit*, that is, having all members, levels, and sectors fit enough to contribute to and draw from a *constant circular flow* of money, information resources, goods, and services. To stifle cross-scale flow, to block thorough circulation by concentrating too much money at the top or letting too little reach lower levels is to cause *economic necrosis*: the dying off of large swaths of economic tissue that will eventually take down the whole system along with the undernourished parts.

Rule #2: *Generously invest in current and future capacities.*

This follows from the fact that long-term vitality depends entirely upon the productive and creative capacities of the entire economic circuit, from top to bottom and all points in between. So, instead of viewing people as costs to be cut, durably vibrant businesses develop the productive capacities of their people, and governments should do the same for the nation as a whole.

Rule #3: *Prosperity requires* **a proper balance of small, medium and large** *organizations.*
This comes from the observation that a wide variety of real-world branching networks—from root systems and river networks to circulatory systems and lungs—have a fractal balance of big and little because this arrangement optimizes circulation across levels, and provides proper-size organizations to meet the needs of each scale. In economic terms, this means we need big banks for large-scale needs and small banks for local needs, and letting big banks gobble up too many small, independent banks damages economic health by reducing monetary circulation to the lower levels.

There is much more to be said, but perhaps the basic idea is clear. Fractal civilization teaches us that *we are 'in this together' economically,* as well as environmentally. It suggests that our next great leap should be towards Free-Enterprise Democracy 2.0—a fractal system of governments *and* economies built "of the people, by the people, and for the people" and designed to deserve the title "adaptive learning system" with sustainable justice, fairness, and prosperity for all. Not only do fairness and integrity become prosperity principles, we suddenly find ourselves with precise mathematical targets and rules for designing vibrant and sustainable economic flows.

It's not just the devil in the details; as healthy fractals demonstrate, good things happen in the details, too. Most economic transactions in the periphery of our world economy require extraordinary coordination and interactivity, just like photosynthesis. These critical peripheral interactions do not only occur in the field of healthcare. They seem to be a rule of healthy life.

Just look at the ingredients on any package and imagine all the machines, robots, and human hands that convey stuff around the globe. Food was moved to some central packaging place, then to your neighborhood, into your shopping bag, and subsequently into your mouth—a system as detailed as any fractal! And pricing depends on global weather patterns, labor conditions, and perhaps a supercomputer algorithm, calculating and pricing over 500 trades per second for a California pension fund. The question is whether the system is working beautifully, moderately well, or not at all.

BIODYNAMICS

Can we step back from this complexity and look at the whole? It's easy to differentiate between a beautifully formed tree and a diseased or deformed one. We must develop the capacity to interpret our world economy as clearly as trees silhouetted in the wintertime sky. Massive trunks, branches, and tiny twigs either reach out in a fine spreading arch or display blunted dead branches, uneven flow, and chaotic structure. They tell a story that can be read by an experienced eye—we might ask, "What went wrong here?"

As our world grows more complex, it also becomes more and more interconnected, like one great tree. When evaluating solutions from the perspective of living systems, what seems at first to be most efficient may lack resilience when something goes wrong. If the whole picture is poorly considered, the devil is not in the details, but in the macro-design. When there are gaps in big-picture thinking, the "devil" will certainly find a home.

In sustainable agriculture, researchers study fractal-like crystallization pictures to determine the qualitative differences between plants grown organically, biodynamically, and chemically. One summer in my early twenties, I visited an agricultural research center in Järna, Sweden, that used a crystallization method to demonstrate qualitative differences in plants grown using different fertilizers.

Like beautiful trees, each crystallization picture had its own character. Both the chemically grown and organically grown plants looked cruder—with less differentiation and fewer refined branches—than the biodynamic sample, which was beautiful and balanced from the trunk all the way to the finest twigs. The organic plant had taken in nitrogen too fast without developing fine root systems—like a venture with too much money being thrown at it and no good plan. Although larger in size, it failed to process the microbiotic life in the topsoil as well as the biodynamic plant. Combining all aspects of the financial world into a few big banks, for example, certainly looks impressive, but too-big-to-fail proved to be unhealthy and unsustainable.

It is imprudent to invest in a world that is profitable in the short term, like a big, perfect-looking, chemically grown plant, but unsustainable in the long term, as suggested by its misshapen crystallization studies. We should already know from the misguided "Green Revolution" that the heavy use of petrochemicals destroys topsoil globally. In India, for example, tens of thousands of farmers tragically committed suicide after government-subsidized chemicals destroyed the fertility of their farms. The microorganisms in the topsoil were starved and the ground poisoned. The short-term thinking behind the real estate boom resulted in "toxic" assets, worthless paper with a trail of malfeasance behind it. How can we keep going down this road?

Only change is certain, yet a little wisdom from the land may serve us well and return us to a healthy economy. Remember, the word "economy" can literally be translated from Greek as "stewarding the household."

Benjamin Franklin's Virtues: Temperance

"Eat not to dullness; drink not to elevation."

The lifestyle of "slow food" was as much a part of French culture in the late 1700s as it is today. Benjamin Franklin showed his flexibility by adopting his hosts' approach to eating and drinking in his older years as ambassador to France. He had avoided alcohol most of his life and was lean and athletically built in earlier paintings, but he returned to the U.S. looking plumpish and a bit rosy-cheeked from his newfound appreciation of wine. Nevertheless we can assume he tried to remain awake, which is the main point of this virtue. "Eat not to dullness; drink not to elevation" is not a form of rigid prohibition, but rather a conscious guideline.

Tempering any activities that affect the ability to think clearly is an obvious prerequisite to raising awareness. At the very least, it is essential for the prudent management of life. Most mistakes are made, destructive arguments are had, crimes are committed, and gambles are lost under the influence of mind-altering substances. But in his wisdom, Franklin does not condemn himself or others for imbibing, but suggests instead this particular form of self-moderation: temperance, a virtue that serves investors well.

CHAPTER 11

HOLISTIC THINKING AND THE THREEFOLD KEY

"A person whose sensory nature manifests the spirituality
of reason, and whose reason manifests the elementary
power of passion, would be a free individuality."
—*Friedrich Schiller*

An epidemic of binary thinking has polarized global society into "haves and have-nots." Fewer than one hundred billionaires own as much wealth as the entire bottom half of the world population combined. It is impossible to imagine that this wealth provides that much more pleasure for them; we are not built to enjoy too much at once. The following chapter suggests a new threefold approach to life and investing that leads to balance and harmony.

Threefoldness is inherent in our human experience, as expressed by our heads, hearts, and hands, in our thinking, feeling, and actions. The ancient ideals of truth, beauty, and goodness parallel our built-in threefoldness: thinking in truth, feeling in beauty, and willing in goodness. These ancient ideals were manifested in democracy through the concepts of liberty, equality, and fraternity, although these were tainted by misuse in the French Revolution and still overused politically to this day. What crowd would not feel inspired by hearing these concepts emphatically spoken out in rousing speeches?

Steiner realized that when applied in the wrong context, for selfish purposes, these ideals backfire and cause harm. He deserves credit for untangling the knot of cynicism that these three ideals sometimes evoke after being misused so horribly. The key is to not muddle them together; one must understand that each works best when constrained to one of the three realms of society:

1. *Liberty*, or freedom, applies best as the governing principle for the sciences, art, and religion, or what might be called the realm of culture;

2. *Equality* serves best as the ideal behind government and justice, or the realm of rights; and

3. *Fraternity* works best in business or the realm of economics.

THE BITTER LEGACY OF THE FOURTEEN POINTS

At the end of World War I, members of the German government asked Steiner to help them prepare his vision for a threefold European society at Versailles. Had the presenters been prepared in time, Steiner's idea could have taken the place of Woodrow Wilson's Fourteen Points. Instead, President Wilson's focus on free trade and the sovereignty of nations set the stage for a continuing world war that in some ways has never ended.

Wilson's simplistic proposal uses the words "freedom" and "equality" in ways that raise contentious issues. Fraternity is not mentioned. Behind the scenes, fraternal organizations with their own agendas were working to muddy the waters with cronyism instead of the collaborative association Steiner envisioned for the European and world economy. The legacy of the Fourteen Points continues to play a part in the growing discrepancy between the rich and poor.

Specifically, Wilson's third point mandates the "removal of all *economic barriers* and the establishment of *equality of trade* conditions." In other words, equality is not fostered in the political realm where it belongs, but an uneven playing field is created for "survival of the fittest" to run *free,* or rampant, in the realm of commerce.

Each of the three components—the cultural life, the life of human rights, and the economic life—can be broken down in turn into three aspects:

- First, the discerning impact of creative thinking;

- Second, the impact of good governance; and

- Third, the ever-present need for mutual understanding while getting things done.

To help contribute to a healthier economy, you can break down your goals again with these same three ideals in mind:

1. To enhance the growth of your portfolio by investing in innovative companies that foster a culture of creative *freedom.*

2. To secure steady income by investing in infrastructure projects and social enterprises that address *equality* of access and *equal* rights.

3. To successfully manage cash for liquidity out of a sense of brother and sisterhood, or *fraternity.*

Think about your neighborhood and keep cash local, or consider short-term notes to microfinance institutions that support entrepreneurs in the global neighborhood. Companies that foster freedom in the creative design of products and services tend to have the most growth potential, while initiatives that consider all stakeholders equally tend to be the most stable for lending. However, freedom and equality have proven to be confusing when used as the primary ideals in the economic sector, and possibly damaging to society as a whole.

Removing all economic barriers allows competitive bullies to rule, while forcing equality in business can lead to mediocre design or dumbed-down standards. Meanwhile, fraternity leads us to care and be cared for like good neighbors, fostering practical associations and a collaborative economic life. The KINS Innovation Networks emphasize that "a deal is a good deal when it is a good deal for everyone."[68] Investing is most meaningful if this principle stands behind it, whether you are investing for growth, income, or simply to preserve your money's buying power.

Free enterprise turns out to be a wolf in sheep's clothing when enterprises focus only on their own isolated agenda of growth. No better are governments that, claiming to be egalitarian, simply take over businesses to increase their own power and control. Steiner's threefold European Society had a chance to develop principles of association for mutual benefit, with less emphasis on ethnicity and rigid borders. Perhaps now is the time to implement this approach.

BASIC INCOME

In 2013, a conference was held in the Goetheanum, the famous building Steiner designed in Dornach, Switzerland, in support of a new basic income initiative. The proposal under discussion was for all Swedish citizens to receive 2,500 Swiss francs a month, whether they were able to work or not—about $2,800 per month, on top of any other earnings. Enno Schmidt, an advocate for the Basic Income, argues that a society where people work only to make money is "no better than slavery."[69]

If people receive just enough money to live on, with no food stamps or other bureaucratic red tape, will they become lazy and less motivated to work? An experiment in Manitoba, Canada, from 1974 to 1978, showed the opposite effect when a basic income was provided over a period of time: people tended to become better educated and healthier, and subsequently more upwardly mobile and less dependent, so government costs decreased overall. The same can be said of the rising middle class in Brazil, which also began with the implementation of a basic income.

Can we envision a world where no one is enslaved by hourly wages, but instead works on behalf of the community and is in turn supported and valued by the community?

The basic income movement is one initiative based on this kind of thinking. Instead, President Wilson's Fourteen Points emphasized the hardening of borders, the separation of ethnicities by mandate, and the empowering of nations. His policies eventually provided free passes to multinational corporations who love to proclaim equal economic rights in the name of "free" trade.

Imagine a world based on Otto Scharmer's ten-point guide (in *italics*; the comments are my own) to Steiner's *Rethinking Economics*:

1. *Economics today has to be based on a world economy, not a national economy.*

Imagine prices determined by representatives of producers and consumers in cooperation, and everything being slave-free, "fair trade," and sustainably produced.

2. *Economic realities today require us to shift from an ego-centric frame of thought to an eco-centric mindset.*

Imagine conscious investors finding, fostering, and funding collaborative financial ecosystems that benefit all stakeholders.

3. *All economic value creation begins with nature and agriculture.*

Imagine thinking of nature not as a commodity to be used up, but as the most generative part of a holistic, living system of values to be cherished and supported.

4. *Wages are not the price for labor, but the price for goods or services.*

Imagine everyone working not for an hourly wage, but to satisfy the basic human need to be recognized as a contributor.

5. *Capital is not money but spirit-in-action.*

Imagine using our capacity to think, innovate, and appreciate resources and relationships to get things done economically.

6. *The problem of our economy is a lack of balance between three types of money (purchase money, lending money, and gifting money), resulting in capital congestion–related speculative bubbles.*

Imagine: (a) Purchase money circulating rather than sitting unproductively in banks, and everyone having enough cash to buy what is needed; (b) bonds and other loan money supporting infrastructure that provides equal access to transportation, energy, clean air, water, and soil; and (c) gifting and investing merging to support innovations of all kinds for a more prosperous future.

7. *Aging of money as a point of leverage.*

Imagine money staying in circulation rather than sitting idle and losing value.

8. *Awareness based self-regulation of the economic process.*

Imagine communities, not just boards, deciding who runs local companies, and imagine managers who see themselves as stewards for the benefit of all.

9. *Imagine every human being would get an average amount of agricultural land.*

Imagine we all learn to grow our own food and feel a partnership in stewarding precious agricultural land.

10. *We need concepts that are more fluid, flexible, and in synch.*
Imagine if, instead of tighter borders and increased bureaucracy, Europe had been shaped by the concept of threefoldness:

- First, cultural life freely differentiated, including flexible educational curriculums with no governmental or commercial intervention.

- Second, governments focused only on equal rights for all human beings.

- Third, cooperative businesses and associations that are inclusive of all consumers and stakeholders, so that pricing is based on what works best for all.

Such fundamental changes are difficult, but not impossible, to imagine. We can work toward them one step at a time. Threefoldness can be applied as a holistic new foundation for all aspects of society, right down to how to work with money. Like the symbiosis of the Native American *three sisters*—corn, beans, and squash—the three sisters of investment are cash, fixed income, and equities, all of which may be woven together in a symbiotic portfolio. For example:

1. The most innovative, or *free*, solutions for equity investments,

2. Loans for improving access and *equal* rights, and

3. The *altruistic* engagement of community banks and very short-term bond ladders that support microfinance.

Mahatma Gandhi was an extraordinarily effective leader who clearly differentiated the way he *invested* his time in three different realms. He described the three spheres of life in this way: his *free* individual deed of nonviolent fasting was supported by his spiritual life; his refusal to accept unjust laws and striving for *equality* was the basis of his political life; and the spinning of home cloth and harvesting of salt from the sea characterized his *altruistic* economic actions on behalf of his fellow Indians.

When applying these principles to money, it can be helpful to think of cash, loans, and equity investments in relation to time. First, since investing is always a leap of faith, it can be considered a gift to the *future* guided by the intuitive insights of *free* individuals. Second, loans can support *equality* in the present by meeting the lender's current income needs, improving access to those aspects of life we all should enjoy as self-evident rights. And third, when making exchanges guided by our imaginative *empathy,* we become grateful for past efforts taken by laborers and appreciate the resources provided by nature.

To achieve long-term sustainability for all, trillions of dollars must be moved away from investments that support short-term prosperity for a few. The polarization that exists between rich and poor stems from our old-fashioned, quantitative-only belief system. Thinking of money as a threefold tool for good, with the entire living world in mind, frees us from an illusory addiction to more money and allows for new solutions that can lead to sustained prosperity.

The balanced investor has the *freedom* to invest in creative innovations that help solve the world's problems. Inspired by the common human needs for clean air, water, and soil, she loans money to provide *equal* access to these wonders of the natural world. And she acts imaginatively with her cash, considering the *impact* of each transaction on the lives of workers and the environment.

Benjamin Franklin's Virtues: Tranquility

"Be not disturbed at trifles, or at accidents common or unavoidable."

The old phrase "penny-wise and pound-foolish" also supports this virtue of financial tranquility. Wise investors will neither squabble over small amounts of money nor squander large sums building castles in the sky. They are likely to tip generously while also sticking to their business and investment plans even in the face of setbacks.

The majority of investors overreact to market "accidents." When markets go up beyond reason, they pile on more, and when markets go down beyond reason, they take money off the table. These emotional reactions are the opposite of tranquility. Instead, one should calmly and rationally do just the opposite: invest when prices are unreasonably low and divest when prices are unreasonably high.

CHAPTER 12:

STEINER AND THE NEW AGE OF HOLISTIC THINKING

"What we say we can't do is in truth what we don't care enough to do." —Johann Gottlieb Fichte

Always focused first on the vital importance of spiritual freedom, Steiner argues that "Free beings are ones who can *will* what they know to be right." In a culture of freedom, work would indeed be separate from income and acts of good will would be chosen freely. We are far from adopting this perspective today because our culture has been built on the concept of "enlightened" self-interest, a refined form of egotism that does not prioritize consideration of the whole. The root of this systemic dysfunction is the valorization of national independence over human collaboration on a global scale.

It is fine to celebrate cultural patriotism or regional pride, but we must recognize that self-centered arrangements, even on a national level, often lead to failure and unhappiness. Selfishness is, in fact, the source of all pain on an individual level. On a global scale, nationalism has been used to justify the pain of isolation and war. How can we move instead toward a global economy based on compassion?

On the way to work one day, I stopped to buy a green smoothie. As I put cash on the counter, both the vendor and I noticed the word *loved* written beautifully in script across the face of a one-dollar bill. I chuckled, for I could easily imagine every transaction as an act of love: one person lovingly providing the product or service and the recipient showing loving appreciation for all that went into it. We are usually too shy or busy to notice the beautiful exchanges of everyday life—but why not enjoy them! It is a matter of intention and expanding one's own awareness.

The same goes for human labor. It makes a tremendous difference when workers are in touch with their labor, when their piece of the puzzle is admired, when they are compensated fairly for what they have done. The need to express and receive gratitude is universal. Unfortunately, most economists consider labor a commodity—just another cost to be cut if possible. Instead of sharing profits with laborers, managers and directors of publicly traded companies spend most of their profits to buy back shares. This exercise manipulates the stock price in their favor so that they can exercise stock options on the most favorable terms, thus increasing the disparity between rich and poor.

All scientists, even economists, have begun to recognize that cold, quantitative mathematical analysis will never explain life as a whole, especially all the complexity of human behavior. We instead get closer to life itself through reverence for the wondrous beauty of nature, be it the geometry of a flower or the light in a child's eyes. This is the foundation for all approaches that are called "holistic."

The fruits of Rudolf Steiner's holistic thinking are well established: Waldorf education considers the "whole" child, and biodynamic agriculture considers the whole farm as an organism. Less well known, perhaps, are the successful initiatives based on Steiner's holistic approach to *money*. Triodos Bank, for example, was founded on Steiner's economic insights. Based in Holland and the U.K., this global bank won recognition as *Fast Company*'s Community Bank of the year in 2009 and continues to provide leadership in new ways of economic thinking.[70]

RSF Social Finance, which financed Waldorf Schools initially, employs "social finance," an approach to lending that the organization continues to cultivate in multiple innovative ways.[71]

With or without Steiner, holistic thinking about money is here to stay. If you watch the introductory videos on Natural Investments or Centerpoint Advisors, for example, you will recognize it immediately.[72,73] More financial professionals are making conscious references to natural systems in ways that are direct and relaxed. Goldman Sachs's relatively tiny initiatives in "social impact bonds" are surprisingly holistic as well.[74]

Benjamin Franklin's phrase "doing well by doing good" is now being spouted off in the most unlikely places. At the Private Equity International Responsible Investment Forum in New York City in 2011, some of the biggest, "baddest" firms in the world were on stage bragging about how many millions they had saved by looking at investments "holistically." They advocated for emergency efficiency strategies and recycling programs because "a penny saved is a penny earned."

CIRCULATION

Another conceptual gift attributable to Steiner is the idea that money is the blood of the community. When healthy, our hearts are constantly sensitive to discord and harmony, and we feel the need to concentrate with discretion on how to make a difference. The heart's rhythm moves from contraction to expansion with a pause in between, like the interval between notes in a melody. When our healthy hearts contract, we feel the need to *just say no* to discord and selfishness. As our hearts expand, we feel the stirring desire to *just do it*—to let the blood flow, to do good in the world and fix what is wrong.

Over the course of our lifetimes, the patterns of our individual personalities are formed as we alternate between these two poles of withholding and taking action. We are shaped by how we apply ourselves in different situations—and especially by how we manage our money.

The global economy continues to be weighed down by indigestible complexity and toxic "assets." Money, the lifeblood of the world community, is not circulating properly, increasing the risk of heart failure. After surviving a heart attack, one might consider changing their lifestyle: reducing stress, eating a lighter diet, exercising and relaxing more, and giving up toxic habits. The planet Earth, ecologically interconnected worldwide, is in danger of heart trouble, especially as the human realm of money is threatened with blockages, bleeding, and even necrosis.

But lifestyle changes only indirectly support the heart; their effects are more immediately visible in the blood. The therapeutic impact of removing stressful, toxic, and indigestible substances can cause blood to become clear and free to do its work.

It is instructive to think of money as being like the blood of a circulatory system. Picture a figure eight, with a heart at the crossing point between two loops. (See diagram on facing page.) Think of the heart as a threshold for key decisions to borrow, lend, gift, or invest. In a healthy economy, research and innovation is first supported by the profits of commerce passing through the "hearts" of socially minded investors, philanthropists, and fund managers. These *intuitive investors* are able to recognize the best minds and the greatest opportunities for creating future value—ideally entrepreneurs and activists working in the clear air of creative freedom. The upper loop in the diagram thus represents the flow of money to new social projects in the form of gifts and investments.

If successful, these ventures eventually hope to scale into commercial operations that require a different kind of money to expand: loan money. This means appealing to the "hearts" of *inspired lenders*, such as community banks, credit unions, and other

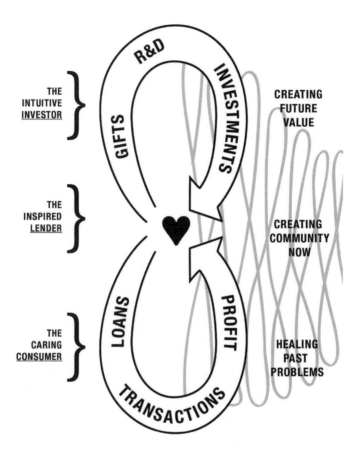

ethical lenders. Imagine a refreshed world in which bankers join local investors to *create community now*, providing the capital necessary to support new infrastructure and initiatives for the common good.

Now the young venture has grown into an established business or nonprofit. Thousands of commercial transactions take place, with either cash or exchange money, as the *caring consumer* takes advantage of products or services offered by the company. Each transaction, if mutually beneficial, profits the buyer as well as the seller. This value creation carries the world forward, *healing past problems* and generating profit for the company's owners and investors.

And so we begin again by considering in our "virtual hearts" how to invest or gift the profit from our commercial exchanges. The evolving cycle continues with the potential for providing well-being and abundance for all.

HEALTHY MONEY CIRCULATORY SYSTEM

Every transaction presents an opportunity for the angel in each one of us to step forward. Care for unproductive members of society—the sick or disabled, the elderly, infants, and the dying—will always, in one form or another, need to be paid for by society. We can see this responsibility either as a burden or as an opportunity to grow as human beings. Similarly in each transaction, at the very personal periphery where money changes hands, both sides can feel either ripped off or privileged and honored.

As investors, we can shift the way markets work by valuing the problem solvers, the innovators, and the truly beneficial products over corporations that grow by wasting natural resources and by creating messes for others to clean up.

Silent gratitude will lead to appreciation of assets, just as it helps the digestion and nourishment of a good meal.

Benjamin Franklin's Virtues: Silence

"Speak not but what may benefit others or yourself; Avoid trifling conversation."

In Franklin's conversation circles, you paid a fine for interrupting or directly disagreeing with one another, and all grudges had to be left at the door. Only remarks that moved the agenda forward were allowed.

There is a tremendous amount of mindless chatter about money. Turn off your TV and pay no attention to gossip about "the market." Instead, quietly focus on the fundamentals and building relationships.

If using money is a form of self-expression, then the virtue of silence reminds us to speak with our money only to benefit others or ourselves. Avoid flaunting wealth or spending with shallow ostentation.

The practice of silence is also a key element of good management. In Otto Scharmer's Theory U. the key idea is for company leaders to let go of their assumptions, then sit in silence before rising up with fresh new ideas to brainstorm together as a team. This could become a part of any family's financial planning practice: come together, drop your agendas, allow for silent refreshment without content, and then allow new visions to arise in brainstorming for common goals. Silence in this way becomes a wellspring of good will.

CHAPTER 13:
THE COOL OF THE DAY

"The eternal mystery of the world is its comprehensibility." —Albert Einstein

Now is the "cool of the day," twilight, a time to reflect on where we are headed. We have gone from industrialization to globalization. Some theorists reckon that we are approaching a "singularity," when robotics, biogenetics, and nanotechnology will reach exponential potential. Will humans, as we know ourselves, become obsolete?

It is a time of reflection and action, the "blessed unrest," as Paul Hawken aptly put it, when all the socially and environmentally progressive NGOs outnumber government and corporate bureaucracies, but have yet to realize their power. The status quo is fraught with inertia and needs serious rethinking. Unprecedented collaboration and infrastructure is required to find, foster, and fund truly beneficial investments, and trillions of dollars will need to be moved in the years ahead. Because business is inherently a response to needs, opportunities will surely abound. Beginning to emerge are mutually inspired associations of gatekeepers that can do the research and due diligence for investors who prioritize the common good.

The three sisters in a healthy financial ecosystem are the same as ever: cash, fixed income, and equities or gifts. In the new money paradigm, however, (1) cash will be spent to pay fairly for *past* work done and materials harvested sustainably, (2) fixed income will stimulate and support *current* solutions, while (3) equities or gifts will encourage intuitive planning for the *future*. We must invest in social enterprises with innovative business models that expect to yield a productive "harvest" of social, environmental, and economic benefit for all stakeholders.

Like members of a CSA garden who want to support local organic farms while also enjoying valuable produce, conscious investors want to support a new, sustainable world economy while also receiving long-term financial benefits. How can this be achieved?

First, cash can be "planted" in rolling ladders of short-term loans to small financial enterprises. These enterprises themselves can provide microloans to entrepreneurs in need, so that cash serves as fuel for a global system of support. The investment is liquid for the investor, as some loans mature monthly, and the interest is variable. In the current economy, this approach is substantially outperforming big-bank money markets.

One example of this alternative approach, MicroVest's Short Duration Fund, contributes both liquidity and higher returns than money markets.[75] Developing world markets have provided Japanese corporations with a similar ladder of microfinance debt. These financial firms, along with TriLinc Global, are looking to create longer-duration microfinance funds that may soon trade on public markets.[76] More such funds are needed to spread the risk and grow the universe of investments with short-term liquidity and social impact.

Second, loans can be "planted" in global nonprofit and for-profit social enterprises. Some of these organizations have innovative business models that allow a 6 percent or better return after fees and expenses, as well as the ability to collateralize or guarantee loans. Such high minimum returns could provide enough income to support the retirement of pensioners. This promising approach requires a collaborative infrastructure that can meet the investment requirements of pension funds and retirement plans, protect assets as much as possible from defaults, and meet critical social and environmental needs.

Loans like these support companies involved in converting thousands of acres to organic production, restoring wilderness, providing green housing for the homeless, and expediting billions in benefits to people in need. Scaling this missing middle in most investment portfolios requires a global infrastructure of due-diligence experts to find the best social enterprises that can provide real collateral.

And third, equity investments can be "planted" for long-term future growth in all sizes of corporate stocks, provided that those stocks promote natural, life-enhancing solutions. Investments can also be made in long-term funds that invest in private equity or venture funds that focus on real assets, such as sustainably managed timber, agriculture, and green real estate.

Imagine cleaning up the waters of the world, building living environments for the poor with materials and designs that save energy and promote community. Imagine small farmers and gardeners who have access to appropriate technology, local food processing, and coordinated distributers, meeting the needs for local organic food globally. Imagine women-owned ventures that prioritize the common good and smart technologies that maximize positive impact.

These are seeds for the world economic garden. The proportion of high-risk and potentially high-return investments must be appropriate for the investors who could absorb such losses should they occur. Successful portfolio management requires a thick skin, tolerance for emotional ups and downs, and a realistic sense of suitable risks.

Associating equity investing with gifting can be helpful because both are done without knowing exactly what the future holds. By embracing the risk and inwardly considering equity investments as gifts to be freely given away, investors can remain peacefully focused on long-term goals and a higher standard of values. This approach does not necessarily imply a lower financial return. Long-term positive returns are inherently a result of products that are worthy of an investor's generous attitude.

Money always represents our "definiteness of purpose," our highest intent, even if many are fooled into thinking that money itself is the purpose. Instead of the exhausting and meaningless strain of "making money," instead concentrate on higher goals that open up new possibilities, industries, and capabilities that would have otherwise never appeared possible.

We are in danger of losing control in the current world drama. The number-one illusion, called money, has fooled us all, and greed is in the driver's seat of a planet that is careening off-track. If we are to succeed in healing the world we love, the world we only see when we stop to reflect, money must become a tool for expressing our highest intentions. The problem is not in money itself but in the limits we place on ourselves.

Positive change can happen only by awakening our hearts and feeling what is possible, by envisioning that "better world." We must follow our individual paths to make both money and change, and be willing to consistently act on that vision and put money down for it. If we are not vigilant, we may head into a virtual jungle, a world filled with the wild animals compelled by fear and greed. Instead, why not use money as the primary tool for positive change, a tool to explore and discover our "higher" selves as protectors of this blue jewel of a planet?

Money can become trapped. Instead, discover who you might become using a new approach to money, one with the highest intention and vision—the love of every member of humanity and each unique soul.

Benjamin Franklin's Virtues: Resolution

"Resolve to perform what you ought; perform without fail what you resolve."

The Divest-Invest Movement is built on the resolution to unload investments that support the fossil-fuel economy and invest in a healthy future. If money is to become an expression of our best intentions, we must follow through on such resolutions. What has always made a difference is the conscience and drive of individuals who are willing to take a stand, to "resolve to do what [they] ought and perform what they resolve." Let's do it!

RESOURCES

AS YOU SOW: www.asyousow.org

As You Sow is made up of investor representatives who believe that greater corporate responsibility is needed before many environmental and human rights issues can be resolved. They communicate directly with corporate executives to collaboratively develop and implement business models that reduce risk, benefit brand reputation, and protect long-term shareholder value while simultaneously bringing about positive change for the environment and human rights.

DIVEST-INVEST: www.divestinvest.org

The Divest-Invest Movement includes foundations currently divesting from fossil fuels and switching to clean energy investments, joining college, health, pension funds and religious organizations doing the same.

FIRST AFFIRMATIVE SRI PERFORMANCE STUDIES: www.firstaffirmative.com/resources-news/news/2013-moskowitz-prize-for-socially-responsible-investing/

Steve Schueth and George Gay have been sponsoring this annual research contest to find the best studies that objectively confirm that positive investment guidelines for people and the planet also benefit the financial bottom line, or, at least, don't hurt.

GREEN AMERICA'S GUIDE TO SRI: www.greenamerica.org/pubs/fph/

Alisa Gravitz and crew have been growing the green economy for decades with catalogs, expos, and this annual guide to socially responsible investing. They now also sponsor the KINS innovation networks, focused initiatives around specific green goals: www.kinsinnovation.org.

GREEN MONEY JOURNAL:
www.greenmoneyjournal.com/calendar/
A great online resource that includes a calendar of events for the SRI world and beyond.

HIP INVESTOR WHITE PAPER ON FOSSIL FREE INVESTING: http://gofossilfree.org/wp-content/uploads/ 2014/05/Resilient-Portfolios-and-Fossil-Free-Pensions-ByHIPinvestor-GoFossilFree-vFinal-2013Oct31.pdf
This link leads to a .PDF file of *Resilient Portfolios and Fossil-Free Pensions*, published by the HIP Investor Press.

IMPACT INVESTMENT STUDY: http://www.sonencapital.com/evolution-of-impact/
Evolution of an Impact Portfolio: From Implementation to Results demonstrates to investors that impact investments can compete with, and at times outperform, traditional asset allocation strategies while pursuing meaningful and measurable social and environmental impact results.

INVESTORS' CIRCLE: www.investorscircle.net
IC is the oldest, largest, and most successful impact investing network for early stage ventures in the world, having propelled over $165 million into 265 impact enterprises dedicated to improving the environment, education, health and community over first twenty years.

MISSION MARKETS: www.missionmarkets.com
The mission of this online transaction platform is "to increase access to impact investments to enable capital to become a catalyst for positive change."

THE PACHAMAMA ALLIANCE: www.pachamamma.org
This group blends indigenous wisdom with modern scientific theory to examine the unintended consequences of humanity's assumptions and to develop new ways of seeing humanity's role on the planet. Their *Awakening the Dreamer, Changing the Dream* symposium (www.awakeningthedreamer.org) is being delivered all over the globe, with thousands of trainers volunteering to present their vision of the future. The underlying purpose is "to bring forth an environmentally-sustainable, spiritually-fulfilling, and socially-just human presence on the planet as the guiding principle of our time."

UN PRI: www.unpri.org
This international group of institutional investors developed the Principles for Responsible Investment, which reflect the increasing relevance of environmental, social and corporate governance issues to investment practices. The process was convened by the United Nations Secretary-General.

US SIF: www.ussif.org
The US Forum for Sustainable and Responsible Investment is an association for professionals, firms, institutions, and organizations engaged in sustainable and responsible investing. US SIF and its members advance investment practices that consider environmental, social and corporate governance criteria to generate long-term competitive financial returns and positive societal impact.

SUSTAINABLE MBA PROGRAMS

The following are some of the current business programs explicitly offering MBA degrees in sustainability. Although many traditional MBA programs have incorporated sustainability-related topics into their curriculum, this list only includes schools offering a specific degree or concentration in sustainability areas:

- Indian Institute of Forest Management, Bhopal, India, offers a PGDFM in Environment Management.

- Aarhus School of Business, Aarhus University, offers a Sustainable MBA option.

- Albers School of Business & Economic, Seattle University, offers a Sustainability Specialization as part of their MBA program.

- Anaheim University offers an online Green MBA degree option.

- Antioch University New England offers an MBA in Sustainability degree.

- Bainbridge Graduate Institute offers an MBA in Sustainable Business, an MBA in Sustainable Systems, and three certificates in sustainable industry topics.

- Blekinge Tekniska Högskola in Sweden offers a Master's in Strategic Leadership Towards Sustainability.

- Bharathidasan University offers an MBA in Environmental Management degree options.

- Brandeis International Business School, Brandeis University, offers a Global Green MBA

- W. P. Carey School of Business, Arizona State University, offers an emphasis in Sustainability as part of their MBA program.

- Clark University offers an MBA in Sustainability

- Colorado State University offers an MBA in Global Social and Sustainable Enterprise.

- Dominican University of California offers an MBA in Sustainable Enterprise.

- Doshisha Business School, Doshisha University, offers a Green MBA certificate/Sustainability focus.

- Duke University offers and MBA with a focus on Energy and the Environment

- Duquesne University offers an MBA in Sustainability degree.

- Golden Gate University offers a concentration option in Managing for Sustainability as part of their MBA program.

- Green Mountain College offers a Sustainable MBA option.

- Haas School of Business, UC Berkeley, offers a concentration in Corporate Social Responsibility to its MBA students.

- INCAE Business School offers a concentration in Sustainable Development to its MBA students.

- Johnson Graduate School of Management, Cornell University, offers a concentration and an immersion in Sustainable Global Enterprise.

- Kenan-Flagler Business School, UNC Chapel Hill offers an MBA@UNC concentration in Sustainable Enterprise.

- Leuphana University Lüeneburg's Centre for Sustainability Management offers an MBA in Sustainability Management.

- Marlboro College Graduate School offers an MBA in Managing for Sustainability.

- Marylhurst University offers an MBA in Sustainable Business.

- MIT Sloan School of Management offers a Sustainability Certificate for MBA and related master's programs.

- Monash University, Australia, offers a Corporate Environmental and Sustainability Management stream within its Master of Sustainability program.

- The Pennsylvania State University offers a "Sustainability and Social Innovation" Concentration for its MBA Program at Smeal College of Business.

- Presidio Graduate School, Alliant International University, offers an MBA in Sustainable Management degree.

- San Francisco State University's College of Business offers an emphasis in Sustainable Business as part of their MBA program.

- Schulich's School of Business offers a specialization in sustainability as part of their MBA program.

- Stuart School of Business, Illinois Institute of Technology, offers a Sustainability concentration to its MBA students and a dual MBA/MS Environmental Management and Sustainability degree.

- Tepper School of Business, Carnegie Mellon University, offers a concentration in Ethics and Social Responsibility to its MBA students.

- Faculty of Management, University of Haifa offers an international MBA program specializing in sustainability.

- Norwich Business School, University of East Anglia, offers an MBA in Strategic Carbon Management.

- University of Exeter offers a One Planet MBA.

- University of Michigan Ross School of Business offers a dual degree program through the Erb Institute for Global Sustainable Enterprise with the School of Natural Resources and Environment.

- University of Oregon Lundquist College of Business offers an MBA with a concentration in sustainability through the Center for Sustainable Business Practices (CSBP).

- University of Vermont School of Business offers a one-year MBA in Sustainable Entrepreneurship (SEMBA); it also offers a three-year JD/MBA degree in sustainable entrepreneurship and environmental law in partnership with the Vermont Law School.

- Zicklin School of Business, Baruch College, offers a major in Sustainable Business Management.

COMMODITIES/MATERIALS:RECYCLED OR SUSTAINABLE

Recycled Metals and Sustainable Produce

To follow the guidelines of the Natural Step, this industrial class can only be satisfied through recycled metals and ecologically sound agricultural production. Avoiding all forms of mining from below the earth's crust is clearly difficult, as many of the best "green technology" solutions for reducing fossil-fuel consumption involve mining silica or mineral sands. China and Australia currently have a monopoly on these resources, and strip-mining practices are causing long-term degradation to vast areas. Mining operations are often temporary, and excavating crews may pack up without reclaiming the land. Corporations must return mined areas to sustainable states after harvesting the materials.

What about gold, the premier commodity, as an alternative for conscious investors? Investors tend to hang on to gold when fearful that other investments will lose value. Gold, never available in abundance, is even less available now. All the gold that has ever been mined (about $8 trillion) could fit into one modest warehouse about ten stories high, forty-five feet across, and fifty yards long. Other cheaper metals are replacing gold in manufacturing. In uncertain times, however, gold seems to offer a sense of meaning and security. As a metal that does not bind with other substances, its chemical properties are distinctive.

Is there a way to find security that does not require stripping mountains and poisoning our waters with cyanide? Unless we search for the pure "gold" within and use money as tool for the good of all, we will continue polluting pristine waters searching for external gold. Diminishing returns are being experienced across the commodities sector, including both gold and oil. Because of the need to process sludge and tar sands, the average barrel of crude oil produces only four barrels of usable oil today, whereas in the past one barrel of crude produced one hundred barrels of usable oil.

Agricultural commodities are also producing less, as petrochemical-based strategies destroy the topsoil and GMOs require more chemicals. Genetically modified seeds typically cannot be kept for the next planting, forcing many small-scale farmers who sell seeds or grow their own out of business.

The entire commodities sector must be reconsidered to ensure a sustainable future. Instead of mining, recycle metals. Current agribusiness is based on monoculture, extracted minerals, petroleum-based spraying programs, and GMOs. Instead, it must change to local, diversified, organic food systems that use local, self-sufficient resources.

More on Materials

The clear mandates of Natural Step are to leave undisturbed the minerals below the earth's crust and to avoid the use of chemical compounds that do not appear in nature. The best approach is to reduce waste and recycle and reuse materials that are already in the biosphere. Biodegradability is another desirable material trait; for example, one should use latex rather than acrylic adhesives and nontoxic, soy-based inks. One company, Ecoverde, has developed a way to add nutrients to used plastic so that micro-organisms in the soil can eat it up, leaving nothing but water and carbon behind. This would end the cycle of recycling! Such innovations need relatively little financial support to change the world.

Recycled materials often contain ingredients that are harmful to skin; for example, recycled paper might contain chlorine and ink, recycled cotton often contains pesticide and dye, and recycled wood might have had toxic lacquers or stains applied to it. These are complex issues. In *Cradle to Cradle: Remaking the Way We Make Things* by William McDonough and Michael Braungart, one study proposed using plastic newspapers printed with soy ink that could be washed off and printed again for subsequent editions, a solution far healthier than recycling newspaper, which wastes massive amounts of water and produces toxic inks as waste.[77]

So how can we best source materials? Here follows a compendium of sources and the concerns associated with each.

Wild Plants

Harvesting from the mountains, deserts, and prairies sounds like a nice green solution for making essential oils, soap, tea, incense, cosmetics, and the like. However, such wild products may not be abundant enough for the scale required. Check whether the businesses defend or preserve the wilderness, pay fair wages to the labor force, and are cautious about the fragility of the ecosystem. Sometimes what sounds positively romantic may in fact cause more harm than good.

Cultivated Materials

Hemp

Cannabis sativa is less than 1 percent tetrahydrocannabinol (THC, the recreational drug content of marijuana) and can be processed into natural threads for clothing. The plant is fast growing, hardy, and has broad leaves that block out sunlight and inhibit competing plants. Hemp does not require herbicides and also does well without synthetic fertilizers or pesticides. The plant can grow to fifteen feet and be harvested three to four months after sowing. Hemp performs best when used as a part of a crop rotation; it has grown in Northern China for over 6,000 years, according to archeological studies.

In 1794, George Washington advised, "Make the most of the hemp seed. Sow it everywhere." The whole plant is useful for food, body care, medicine, textiles, and many kinds of paper. In fact, hemp plants produce four times more cellulose per acre than timber, and, because of its creamy color, hemp requires less bleach when processed into paper. Hemp can also be used as a biomass fuel and to manufacture biodegradable plastics such as composite parts for cars and skateboards.

Hemp has not been legal to grow in North America since 1938 (except when it was required to support WWII) and remains listed on the "Controlled Substance Act." Hemp textiles, however, are allowed and are increasingly popular. Canada resumed growing hemp in 1998, and the plant is currently grown in Romania, China, France, and Australia.

Bamboo

Bamboo is a type of grass with over 1,300 species, each exhibiting subtle differences in hardness, thickness, and grain structure. Often available locally, fast-growing bamboo plants grow wild in an invasive way that must be managed. The parent plant develops new stems every year, and stems can be harvested after five years in a mature forest without decreasing the size of the forest. Regular harvesting improves growing power.

Bamboo is long lasting and strong with sturdy shoots; Thomas Edison used bamboo as rebar in his pool—which still hasn't cracked. Bamboo can be used for paper, pulp, housing, construction, and flooring, as well as for textiles. It may be preserved by smoking and can be sealed with nontoxic substances. Some glues used in bamboo flooring may be toxic, and it is important to consider other manufacturing concerns as well.

Trees

Trees provide an important renewable material—wood. Members of the Menominee tribe in Wisconsin practice harvesting only when a tree starts to decline in health, for example, when signs of red ring rot appear. The best trees are preserved, thus creating a healthy old-growth forest.

Cellulose, a polysaccharide, is the main element of all living plant tissues and fibers. *Polysaccharides* are polymeric carbohydrates, organic compounds that have organic chemical formulas including carbon and water. Polysaccharides store energy and serve as structural components in living beings. Cellulose, the structural component in plants that makes wood convertible to paper, paperboard, and cardboard, can be reprocessed in postconsumer or recycled products. Cellulose from wood is also used in the production of cellophane, rayon, water-soluble adhesives and binders, wallpaper paste, thickeners, stabilizers, and even to prevent caking in processed foods. Cork grows on special trees that are not harmed by the harvesting of the bark.

The main ecological concern is whether the wood products come from sustainably grown timber. The certification process for sustainable forestry may differ greatly in terms of do's and don'ts. The sustainable forest funds Ecotrust Forest Management and Lyme Timber both approach foresting in different ways as the science of silvaculture continues to evolve.[78,79] Ultimately the net effect is an increase of green jobs and eco-diversity, and the process of natural selection conserves ecosystems and leads to future mature wood of extraordinary value.

Palm Oil

About one third of plant-based oil consumption comes from palm oil. (Soybean oil is a top competitor.) Eighty-nine percent of crude palm oil is produced in Malaysia and Indonesia. Palm oil has the highest yield per hectare when compared to all other plant oils. Because the trees are highly productive for twenty-five years, it is also the cheapest plant-oil source. The U.S. is a top importer, along with India, China, and Eastern Europe, and about half the goods on grocery-store shelves contain palm oil, including chocolate bars.

The kernel oils are also used to make soap, cosmetics, and detergents. Meal from the plant is made into palm kernel cake as a "low-cost" supplement for animal feeds. One ton of fresh palm fruit bunches results in 20 percent oil, 20 percent bunch matter (sometimes burned for biomass-based power), and 60 percent waste effluent, which is sometimes dumped into the water untreated, causing fish to die.

Other environmental issues surround the destruction of bio-diverse rainforests for monoculture palm oil plantations. Logging companies have been known to convince communities that logging is necessary to finance palm oil plantations, then leave without notice, taking the profits. The farmers who rush in to claim the newly opened land often apply over twenty different synthetic pesticides, herbicides, and insecticides, causing water and land health issues. Forests are frequently burned and cleared, destroying hunting grounds and smallholder farms, not to mention habitat and biodiversity (tigers, orangutans, elephants, rhinoceros, and countless others).

Plant oil production may seem to promise social benefits, but it can end up creating a concentration of land-ownership and a loss of community control. Pressure for commercial success encourages the use of genetically modified strains, and most plant-based oils today come from possibly untested GMO strains. On the positive side, the oil is free of "trans fats" and is a better alternative to other trans-fatty oils. A simple cold press of the fruit is the healthiest process for obtaining the oil, with no further processing necessary.

Fortunately, the Roundtable on Sustainable Palm Oil was initiated through a partnership between the palm oil industry and the World Wildlife Federation.[80] This "multi-stakeholder body" provides strong guidelines for palm oil production, including:

- No burning for land clearing

- Watercourse protection by buffer zones of natural vegetation

- Integrated pest management to reduce pesticide use

- Proper treatment of mill effluent and other wastes

- Respect for customary land-use rights of local communities

- Transparency in environmental and social policies

Their independent monitoring and verification can be followed at www.rspo.org.

Manufactured Materials

Plastics

Plastics, generally manufactured from petrochemicals mined from below the earth's crust, should be avoided as much as possible. That said, there are a variety of characteristics that distinguish different types of plastic from one another. Here are some facts to note:

- Dyes, fillers, and other additives used in plastics are often difficult to remove; additives are less widely used in beverage containers and plastic bags for improved recyclability.

- Plastics are often recycled into different kinds of plastic, and products made from recycled plastics are often not recyclable. (Technology developed by companies like Ecoverde allows us to complete the cycle: the carbon that once grew in primeval forests, became fossil fuel, and was finally processed into plastic can now return to the soil as carbon again!)

- PET (postconsumer polyethylene) products are sorted by color, cleaned, crushed, chopped, and pressed into bales; flakes can be spun into polyester threads and yarn.

- HDPE (high-density polyethylene) can be recycled and is said to be the most-often recycled plastic. It is down-cycled into plastic lumber, tables, roadside curbs, benches, trash receptacles, and rulers.

- PVC (polyvinyl chloride) is difficult to recycle on a large scale.

Plastic packaging used for deodorant, contact solution, plastic bags, Styrofoam cups, and other non-biodegradable materials can take hundreds of years to decompose, polluting our drinking waters and land. Conscious investors and consumers prefer packaging that is natural, biodegradable, or recyclable, in that order. The burning of plastics, along with the widespread use of Agent Orange as a home garden and agricultural herbicide, has polluted the ground with dioxins, major hormonal disrupters in animals and probably also in humans.

Bio-plastics that do not compete with food sources are a good alternative. If bio-plastics are mixed with plastics, however, the reclaimed plastic unfortunately is not recyclable—for example, Coca-Cola's PlantBottle. Bio-plastics are often corn- or sugarcane-based and take up land that could be used to grow food. Surprisingly these plastics can be hard to compost. Additives can accelerate biodegradability, but may be toxic. More R&D is needed.

Quantitative evidence regarding the effects of wearing recycled plastic, polyester, or polyester-blended textiles is inconclusive. Nonetheless, many people find that natural materials feel substantially different qualitatively, like the difference between food warmed by vibrating cells in a microwave and food warmed in a wood-fired oven. Some people believe that children particularly benefit from the breathable quality of organic cottons, wools, and linens.

Fertilizer

Fertilizers are preferably obtained from organic sources—leaf mulch, food waste, and animal waste. Food that is not treated with synthetic chemicals will be most nutritious and is generally sweeter to the taste. Human feces contain many toxins, including heavy metals, and in general should not be composted. The USDA pressed to include human sludge as an approved substance in the definition of organic fertilizer, but this concept was wisely voted down.

Artificial fertilizers were initially developed using leftovers from the production of nitrogen-based explosives in WWI. These chemical compounds are firstly detrimental because their precursors are extracted from the earth. More importantly, chemical fertilizer is fed to plants directly, meaning that the topsoil is bypassed and becomes inert and depleted, while the food is prevented from absorbing the complex micronutrients that thrive in good soil. Every year, millions of tons of topsoil blow away due to poor soil management and the heavy use of damaging chemicals, causing desertification. Even on organically farmed land, if plants have been fed directly with un-ripened manure, the nutrient value of the food, not to mention the taste, will diminish dramatically.

Fluoride is an element essential to the production of synthetic fertilizer, chemical weapons, and nuclear weapons. Extracted in the mining of phosphates, fluoride-based byproducts are toxic. This waste product was once widely used for rat poison, and before that was a main ingredient in bomb production during WWII. Since the 1950s, the U.S. has spent about $35 billion to clean up stockpiles of chemical weapons made primarily of fluoride; this cleanup effort continues but remains incomplete.

Fluoride is contained in sodas and toothpastes and was a main ingredient in the production of the Syrian chemical weapons arsenal. In the United States, fluoride is dumped into most big-city water supplies to try to halt tooth decay—with the exception of Portland, Oregon, where a referendum called the practice to a halt. Fluoride is not allowed in most of Europe due to its questionable efficacy: Too much fluoride exposure might damage the teeth of children, and one study suggests that high fluoride levels could be a factor in lower IQs.

Ending industrial agriculture could be the first step in a comprehensive peace plan. No more fluoride production to worry about, and good local food for all! Leave this, the most reactive mineral, in the ground where it belongs.

Instead of being depleted, soil should be enlivened by crop rotation, composting, and the use of vital natural sprays. Instead of insecticides, beneficial insects such as ladybugs can be introduced to eat the larvae of pests. Encouraging birdlife is also smart; ducks especially love slugs and don't damage the garden. Small-scale ecological agriculture is growing in popularity through Community Supported Agriculture and the Slow Money movement. We need to encourage farming practices that are ecologically sound.

CONSUMER STAPLES: SUSTENANCE OR NOURISHMENT

The summary goal of consumer staples, products required for daily life, is to provide *sustenance* or *nourishment*. Physical sustenance includes the basic food, clothing, and shelter required to sustain the physical body. Emotional or "soul" sustenance requires food products that are local or at least fair trade. Such products generate a feeling of connection based on where the food comes from, who is involved, and how they are paid. This meets a need to participate in a greater, more caring whole. On the highest tier is biodynamic food that nourishes the body, helps to sustain dynamic thinking, and strengthens and engages the will.

In an economy that prioritizes the common good, we can invest in consumer staples that truly nourish the human being on all levels while providing workers with living wages and consumers with affordable quality food.

CONSUMER DISCRETIONARY: ERGONOMIC

Lifestyles of Health and Sustainability, or "LOHAS," has become an important term for discerning shoppers. Using Max Neef's framework of physical, emotional, and spiritual requirements, the underlying needs might be security, leisure or relaxation, and identity or meaning. "Ergonomic" is one useful term for thinking about what products might serve the LOHAS market. What is needed for a comfortable home? Lighting that enhances, inviting natural materials, furniture that fits and supports, products with a personal touch made by fairly paid artisans, and artwork that awakens or provides healing.

The antithesis would be stuff that ends up in the landfill because it was unneeded and unable to be composted or recycled.

ELECTRONICS AND TELECOM: RECYCLED AND REUSED

Common toxins in electronic equipment include PVC, mercury, solvents, flame retardants, lead and other heavy metals. But electronics can be designed to incorporate nontoxic materials so that the e-waste problem doesn't occur in the first place. Electronic items can be designed so that glass, plastic, copper, aluminum, silver, gold, and steel can be restored and reused. This keeps the toxins out of dumps and landfills and eliminates the risk of exportation to a "developing country" for hazardous processing, potentially by slaves or children.

Heather White, a Network Fellow at Harvard's Edmond Safra Center for Ethics, and head of New Standards, has recently documented the unnecessary use of benzene, which is highly carcinogenic, to clean screens on smart phones because it dries faster than water.[81] The result is an alarming incidence of leukemia in young workers in Chinese factories. White's exposé, along with media support from Green America and others, recently lead to Apple's decision to stop using these harmful chemicals in their production facilities.

Recycling systems need to be monitored: some workers may not wear protective gear, while other might recover only valuable parts while burning or trashing the rest. Manufacturers should ideally be responsible for taking back products at the end of their lifespans. This gives manufacturers a mandate to design products to be longer lasting, less toxic, more recyclable, and modular. Electronics can also be designed to be more energy efficient, thereby decreasing dependence on fossil fuels.

A flat world based on virtual reality creates huge cultural effects, both positive and negative. Ironically, although connectivity distributes information universally, it may increase an individual's sense of isolation, or at least decrease their need for face-to-face contact.

Also, data are beginning to indicate long-term effects of the ever-increasing electromagnetic radiation we have invited into our lives. Are we slowly microwaving our brain cells? Electronic devices give off electromagnetic waves, disrupting the body's natural energy flow and functionality. Radio-frequency identification devices are available to track these effects, as are esoteric accessories for creating a healthy bio-field to counteract the negative frequencies. Some of these devices are supported by peer-reviewed data.

When thrown away—and there is no real "away"—electronics pollute our land, water, ecosystems, and future generations. Unfortunately obsolescence is to be assumed as the speed of technological change continues to accelerate. For this reason, businesses that collect and recycle e-waste in a humane way are extremely valuable.

HEALTHCARE: WELLNESS AND PREVENTION

Dispensing chemical compounds to fight illness has become an addictive practice that, like all addiction, is self-perpetuating. For many in the developed world, the new normal is to be on drugs. As the LOHAS movement grows, more people are pushing forward a new consciousness of personal responsibility for wellness. Some illnesses indicate imbalances and the need for change, and they should be taken as wakeup calls instead of problems to be solved with chemicals.

Years ago, a consultant who came in to Legg Mason kicked off his presentation by asking, "Do you love your jobs? If not, your body has all the makings of illness inside you to help you exit!" Therapies should respect our natural ability to heal. Physically handicapping conditions may require direct physical support and critical care, while serious chronic illness may require serious intervention balanced with holistic systems of support.

Escape Fire: The Fight to Rescue American Healthcare (2012), a documentary on the American healthcare system, begins and ends with a powerful image—a fire is intentionally set to burn a safe haven for fire fighters in the middle of a wildfire. Our healthcare costs, like a wildfire, are out of control with devastating results. The more we spend on drugs and expensive equipment, the less healthy we seem to become.

Universal insurance will not entirely improve matters. Physicians should be paid based on the health of their patients, and alternative practices like acupuncture, healing nutrition, preventive exercise, and meditation regimes should be recognized and supported by investors. These natural and homeopathic remedies can be seen as proactive approaches for health, like an escape fire for the industry.

FINANCIALS: COMMUNITY

Like big-box retail, "too big to fail" banks are among the biggest leeches of local capital, removing it from circulation to fatten the wallets of faraway corporate managers. The "move your money" movement awakened the public consciousness to this fact, leading billions back to local community banks and credit unions. Switzerland has used a local currency for business-to-business exchanges for almost a century, stabilizing the country even in times of great turmoil. "Slow Money" proponents are developing ways to finance local food systems beyond the one-farm-at-a-time CSA model. Nature-based businesses, like those supported by Accelerating Appalachia in Asheville, North Carolina, are the beneficiaries of "patient capital" that is responsible for the recent growth of artisan cheeses, beers, and breads all over this country.[82]

Investors who prioritize community building will avoid multinational banks, instead investing in banks that focus on local needs, keeping local money local. Unfortunately, several such banks are struggling; greedy to expand, franchise banks have swallowed up many local banks through acquisition. On the other hand, investors who want to think globally and act locally in remote geographies can take advantage of microfinance institutions that are beneficial in other parts of the world.

MicroVest Short Duration Fund is a great example of an innovative and beneficial approach to cash management. A ladder of short-term notes that come due at regular intervals, MicroVest provides capital to financial institutions in some 40 countries that have been vetted for financial stability and, more importantly, for the institution's deep knowledge of and trust from local entrepreneurs. Other such creative platforms should be developed to increase the circulation of money for the common good both locally and globally.

Altogether a healthy focus for the financial industry is to maximize capital resources in order to carve a better world. This can be done through investing in creative innovation, lending for infrastructure, and monetary systems that facilitate access to capital for all. These are the keys for a healthy global community and for healthy local communities globally.

INDUSTRIALS: ZERO WASTE

The Dow Jones Industrial Average comprises the thirty largest manufacturing corporations in the world. Now, companies that provide virtual services, like Google and Baidu, its Chinese counterpart, have joined this elite group. For the purposes of diversifying a portfolio, the industrial sector is in fact the manufacturing sector. The question now becomes this: What large-scale manufacturing company is not dependent on large-scale extraction of minerals, including petrochemicals and metals? Very few, it might seem. Some large-scale companies do manufacture goods out of recycled metals, sustainable lumber, or recycled products. The problem with scale is the scale of waste, including waste in the production process itself.

If a product is not wasted, then it may be used again and again, proving it is designed to meet a real need. It must be reusable, renewable, and improve one's quality of life. Otherwise, it will just be "thrown away." A product that does not meet these three criteria will likely add to the piling up of waste. Therefore, one phrase in particular is most important for evaluating the industrial sector: ZERO WASTE. Zero waste in the manufacturing process, including the use of human potential, zero waste by only providing products essential to life, and zero waste in the sense of durability, renewability, and restorability.

INFORMATION TECHNOLOGY: EMPOWERMENT

If the Gutenberg press was essential to the impact of the Renaissance, spreading knowledge to the elite, in the last twenty years the Internet has made a world of information accessible for the masses. If knowledge is power, then the Internet gives even remotely situated individuals access to power.

When diversifying an investment portfolio to include IT, the social or environmental researcher might first want to research whether an IT company is making an effort to reduce its "carbon footprint" in terms of the energy required to build products or maintain its servers. The second prerequisite is to provide sufficient security and not abuse user information or allow hackers easy access for identity theft. Most important in this sector, however, is how well the IT company addresses the human needs for participation, creativity, and the freedom of customization. The company culture can maximize its scalability and impact by emphasizing creativity. This can be achieved through open-source design, user-friendly equipment, and protocols that encourage collaboration.

REAL ESTATE: GREEN AND SUSTAINABLE

Ideally, real estate benefits us on a physical, emotional, and spiritual level through the use of beautiful, natural materials, natural lighting when possible, and passive or zero-energy systems. Timber and other sustainably grown materials add to this picture of health and comfort. Simple improvements like double-paned glass windows can be extraordinarily efficient ways to improve ambience by adding light and warmth. It is possible to purchase nontoxic paints and sealants, avoid formaldehyde-based glues for laminates, and, rather than toxic insulation, invest in new natural insulation products composed of recycled cellulose. Encourage the use of local, readily available materials that are natural and long lasting, such as for cob buildings made of clay and plant materials.

Water efficiency can be improved with composting toilets, waterless urinals, or low-flow faucets and toilets. Increase insulation by using living walls and roofs, and capture and make better use of rainwater, or at least avoid excessive runoff. The shape and position and even the color of rooms can deeply affect the well-being of the inhabitants; consider positioning buildings to best benefit from sun and currents of fresh air.

The proximity of real estate to public transportation, shopping, and mixed-use venues is also critical, as are community spaces and natural landscapes. Trees have been shown to be the biggest single deterrent to crime in a neighborhood! Community property ownership models must be further developed to allow for low-income families in particular, but all urban and rural dwellers should have a sense of long-term stewardship, security, and identity. Cohousing and land trusts are part of this experimental phase and should be observed and supported.

SERVICES: ESSENTIAL NEEDS

The purpose of this broad sector, which includes most of the jobs in our modern economy, is to serve human and environmental needs. Nothing is actually produced, so the investment impact is dependent on the service provided to clients. The impact of insurance, for example, can be tremendously beneficial, but a great proportion of applicants are turned away. In his book *Deadly Spin*, the insurance industry whistleblower Wendell Potter exposes the fact that many insurance companies are actually designed to avoid being of service.[83]

Here are a few other examples from the service sector:

- *Consulting services*. Quality assurance, job training, and call centers are all parts of this sector. Environmental consultants should be engaged if they genuinely work for the environment's benefit, rather than catering to the wishes of corporations that want to avoid regulation.

- *Trading and other online transactional platforms* are services that could provide more efficiency in the market and eventually lead to markets that take human values into consideration. One example is carbon trading, which reduces greenhouse gas emissions by making them more expensive. Local trading systems and associations that set fair prices for local goods are another. We should support these efforts when we can.

- *Data centers* make the huge electronic world of the Internet possible. These systems run constantly, powered by at least fifteen energy plants in the U.S. alone. Superefficient equipment is a key differentiator in this category.

- *Advertising*, if viewed as a service, should be designed to teach for the common good rather than to manipulate for self-interested profit. Hazel Henderson sponsors an annual contest, the EthicMark Award, to acknowledge advertising that uplifts society and the human spirit.

- *Emergency services* are generally part of the healthcare system, but some global initiatives strive to improve the access to care through such services. Again, investors should assess the actual cost-to-benefit ratio of the business model for the clients who make use of it.

- *Environmental Services* provide expert preventive consulting and damage control, as well as environmental cleanup services.

TRANSPORTATION: EFFICIENT MOBILITY

Until the Carter years, the availability of fossil fuels seemed endless. Few thought to ask how much of this black-smoke pollution the earth and its inhabitants could tolerate. Our dependence on fossil fuels in the transportation sector has prompted a continual search for oil, the development of greater fuel efficiencies, and other solutions completely divorced from fossil fuels. Human beings around the world must find ways to meet one another regardless of geography in an efficient, comfortable, and safe way without poisoning the air we breathe.

Efficient mobility is what is called for. Mobility is essential to humans as social beings. Efficient mobility includes efficient use of materials, efficient sources of renewable fuels, and ultimately the efficient use of energy.

ENERGY AND UTILITIES

The energy and utilities sector presents us with the most pressing reasons to rethink and moderate our actions in the investment realm. If we don't, future generations will not experience the world as we know it.

When considering an energy investment, one must ask three questions: Does the source emit carbon into the atmosphere? Is the source limited or renewable? And finally, is it efficient, making it less expensive both in terms of financial and environmental cost?

It is said that a butterfly might set a process in motion that could cause a storm overseas. As consumers of energy, when we turn on a light or adjust the thermostat, the effect is much greater than a butterfly flapping its wings. On a physical level, the flip of a switch often increases the need for oil extraction, natural gas fracking, or coal strip-mining. But instead, the same switch could increase the demand for wind, solar, algae-based bio-fuels and smart grids.

Loren Eiseley's classic treatise *The Immense Journey* posited the idea that humanity's evolutionary purpose is *consciousness*. Each time we flick a switch unconscious of how it all works and the necessary consequences, we increase the likelihood of *devolution*— that humanity's general consciousness will devolve. Instead of becoming the "crown of creation," as Loren Eiseley put it, humans will devolve to the level of the machine. Our dependence on dirty energy is bad for our souls, and we feel it. Clean, smart systems support our evolving consciousness and provide a sense of security and freedom. If we invested in and developed positive renewable resources, they could already provide twenty-four times the energy we currently use.

Each time you use technology, think back through the chain of interlinked facets back to the actual source of energy instead of mindlessly taking it for granted. For example, as Bill McKibben has often pointed out, the use of electric cars is no big improvement if they are dependent on electricity from coal.

Nonrenewable Resources

Natural Gas

Natural gas, or methane/propane, has the lowest hydrogen-to-carbon ratio of the fossil fuels, which makes it the "cleanest burning" with little to no carbon residue. The nitrogen left over from natural gas is a major feedstock for artificial fertilizer. Microscopic organisms create natural gas as part of their metabolic process in conditions where no oxygen exists.

Natural gas extraction can pollute water with heavy metals: when drilling deep in the ground, aquifer water comes out first, bringing heavy metals that can then run into lakes and rivers. When natural gas is drilled in the U.S., methane, a greenhouse gas more potent than carbon dioxide, is released directly into the atmosphere. Natural gas is highly explosive and can escape from high-pressure underground pipelines to create explosions and environmental disasters.

Shale gas drilling can pollute community waters; this drilling requires a lot of water and chemicals to facilitate the underground fracturing process that releases natural gas. This results in large quantities of contaminated water that must be kept in above-ground pools, trucked to another state, or injected back into the earth.

Petroleum

Petroleum is the most common source of energy in the world, from thick motor oil to diesel and gasoline to kerosene. Ironically, all petroleum comes from the breakdown of primeval forests that once harnessed the energy of the sun through photosynthesis! The problem after all this time is that not all of the stored energy goes into producing power—much is wasted in exhaust, contributing greatly to global warming.

Nuclear

"Splitting the atom," or nuclear fission, converts radioactive uranium and plutonium into nuclear fuel. Both elements are dangerous and have extraordinary shelf lives: plutonium is theoretically lethal in microscopic doses for more than 250,000 years after it is used. Building nuclear plants is prohibitively expensive and dangerous, as is well known from the disasters at Three Mile Island, the Vermont Yankee plant, Chernobyl, and most recently the Fukushima Daiichi disaster in Japan.

Aging parts, design problems, and the question of what to do with radioactive waste supersedes the fact that the emissions from nuclear reactors seem to be relatively pure. The vulnerability of plants to military or individual violence provides another argument for halting the development of nuclear power. There is, however, hope that a low-energy nuclear reaction can be developed to provide endless power with no radioactive waste. We'll see.

Geothermal

Geothermal energy can be used to regulate temperature in individual homes or commercial buildings by accessing the solar energy absorbed at the surface. Energy Star compressors and ground-source heat pumps can be used to maximize the heat transfer. In locations where temperatures are at extremes in the summer or winter, ground-source heat pumps are the most energy-efficient and environmentally friendly temperature-regulation strategy for individual homes and buildings.

For generating electricity, heat from the earth can be captured by drilling deep down to access the heat produced from the radioactive decay of minerals. However, this process can release CO_2, hydrogen sulfide, methane, and ammonia, elements responsible for causing acid rain and global warming. Hot water released may contain toxic chemicals such as mercury, arsenic, boron, and antimony. These geothermal plants are usually located along plate tectonic boundaries and can affect land stability. In Switzerland, the operations of the Basel geothermal plant were suspended after more than 10,000 earthquakes, some measuring 3.4 on the Richter scale, occurred in the first six days of water injection.

Enhanced geothermal systems are designed to extend geothermal potential beyond plate boundaries to almost anywhere on earth. First a well is drilled four to ten kilometers deep and water is injected to fracture the rock beneath, creating thousands of small pathways for the water to flow and be heated. The hot water and steam are pumped back to the surface to power turbines and generate electricity, then recycled back into earth to bring up more hot water and steam in a closed loop. But heavy metals and toxins are released from deep within earth's crust. What happens to the toxins that come back up with the water?

Additionally, geysers and hot springs, often sacred places for indigenous peoples, can be destroyed if geothermal power plants are created on top of them. We do not favor geothermal utilities for all of these reasons.

Renewable Resources

Renewable resources include wind, solar, algae, fuel cells, hydro-electric, waste-to-energy, and bio-fuels. One key issue is how to best store, transmit, and share renewable energy through a smarter grid. Modular standalone energy systems do not require the grid at all. This is the new trend, and there are currently over 200,000 new homes in the U.S. that are entirely energy self-sufficient.

Solar

Solar provides a renewable source of power by capturing the sun's energy with photovoltaic and thermoelectric technologies. Many areas use solar power efficiently to preheat water for heating or washing. A few innovations for generating solar electricity include:

- Thermo-solar, which uses mirrors to focus the sun's energy to a central receiver, generating steam that powers electric turbines.

- Thin-film solar, which is thinner than a piece of paper. A special foil layer can be installed on conventional roof shingles to generate electricity for the home.

- Tracking systems that follow the sun throughout the day.

- Batteries to store energy.

- Inverters that convert DC power produced by solar cells to AC power for the utility grid.

- Ceramic and glass solar modules that collect and store the sun's heat.

Space-based solar, which involves costly satellites with the potential to beam solar energy seven times as intense as the sun to earth with microwave systems. This approach is risky and not cost effective. It is an example of overkill since the sun already sends enough energy for all our needs. One new concept being developed is the solar road. Instead of paving roads with tar waste, we could create sturdy solar modules we can drive on, with the capacity to melt the snow and ice and become a door-to-door grid for everything, including electric vehicles.

Some issues with solar include the dependence on mined silica, the use of mineral sands in battery systems, the ecological effect of blanketing large areas with solar panels, questions of durability and cost of replacement, and the effect of materials that cannot be recycled.

Plant Algae

Plant algae that can be turned into renewable biodiesel may be the most promising new development, though it is yet to be commercially successful. The amount of space required is minimal in relation to the potential energy generation. Exxon is experimenting with the manipulation of algae genes, so there may be unintended consequences in terms of unknown characteristics of GMO algae. Experiments with algae production are being conducted alongside natural-gas sites so that CO_2 and heat waste can be used to warm and nourish the algae beds. Watch this one.

Fuel Cells

Fuel cells take a highly volatile gas, hydrogen, from water and convert its chemical energy directly into electricity, emitting only water and heat as byproducts. This provides continuous DC power, similar to batteries, but these cells are capable of generating power as long as fuel is supplied, whereas batteries are limited to the energy stored within. Since many buildings are now powered by fuel cells, the systems are well proven. South Korea has installed the world's first large-scale fuel cell utility plant, powered by water and exhausting only water.

It is interesting to note that liquid hydrogen, which is very safe to transport, can be produced by any kind of turbine that produces electricity as its main function. Picture windmills on the North Sea generating electricity for local use and hydrogen to truck all over Europe for fuel cells! California's state government recently passed a bill to fund hydrogen fuel filling stations for the new fuel cell cars.

Wind

Wind technologies have been around for centuries and continue to grow as a major renewable power source. Some relatively new designs are useful on a small scale, such as helical windmills, which we favor because these structures can take wind from any direction and can be put on buildings for off-the-grid use.

Most windmills, however, are huge towers that can dominate scenic vistas, disrupt habitats and migratory routes, affect water drainage patterns, and endanger bats, raptors, and other birds, including endangered species. Offshore wind turbines can disturb dolphins and whales. Wind turbines also generate low-frequency electromagnetic waves and can cause sickness for those who live nearby, in some cases forcing them to sell or vacate their homes.

On the other hand, wind farms are often the best alternative energy source in certain geographies and can serve as community-based sources of revenue for local owners. The practical issue is storage capacity and transmission through the grid without losing energy. Again, the issue of rare earth minerals in the battery systems is a problem. Local use seems best.

Biomass

Waste-to-energy can turn a problem (waste) into a solution (energy) by channeling biogas or burning waste wood. This form of "reverse photosynthesis" sounds good, but biomass burning makes up 30 percent of global CO_2 emissions, according to NASA's Dr. Joel Levine.[84]

We suggest the following guidelines for using biomass cleanly:

1. For feedstock, use wasteland instead of farmland, and use abundant weeds, not cultivars.

2. Transform solid waste into fuel rather than polluting the air by burning.

3. Focus on algae, which can be grown efficiently in small spaces, or halophytes, which are prolific on desert wasteland when irrigated with seawater.

Ethanol and Bio-Fuel

The use of ethanol can be ethically considered if it does not take good agricultural land away from food production or require the use of heavy agricultural chemicals. Cellulosic ethanol, for example, can be created from prairie grass, wood chips, or sawdust. It can also be created from waste feedstock or halophytes grown with salt water on wastelands.

Biodiesel is a renewable bio-fuel that is obtained from the chemical reaction of methanol or bio-ethanol with plant oils, such as rape, sunflower, soy, palm, and jatropha oils. It does not contain much sulfur, and, in contrast with oil-derived diesel, produces fewer greenhouse gases (CO_2, among others), carbon monoxide, and other polluting particulates when burned for fuel or used in a generator. Waste vegetable oil on a small local scale can be obtained from local restaurants.

To give this idea some perspective, about 9,000 liters of water are needed to grow the 4,000 liters of soy, corn, or sugarcane required to produce one liter of biodiesel. Other plants make more efficient use of water, but using good agricultural land for energy production may never make sense.

Hydroelectric

Hydroelectric dams and their accompanying transmission lines can ruin rivers, flood biologically diverse territories, and displace local peoples dependent on their ecosystems for self-sufficient living. In geographies rich in moving water, however, small-scale or even mini-hydroelectric power generation captures energy in the flow of water and mitigates the environmental and displacement concerns of large-scale hydroelectric operations. However, this is still a disturbance of an ecosystem to avoid if possible.

Wave and Tidal

Wave and tide energy generation utilizes the power of waves as a source of renewable energy; buoys are used as a mechanism for enabling the power generation. These systems can have a negative effect on ocean life, as the bulk of the technologies can be underwater. This source of energy is promising—Scotland recently launched the world's largest tidal turbine—but it must be monitored carefully.[85]

Micro-Power

The decentralization of power systems is compelling for many reasons, not the least of which is the brittleness and lack of resiliency in systems that all fail at once! It is important to look at technologies that can be modular and local as well as renewable. The utility companies should find ways to get into this decentralized game, or they might lose out long term.

REFLECTIONS ON GOLD

ITS HISTORY, AND ITS ROLE IN THE ECONOMY

Since metals have been such high-performing commodities in recent years, an extra word about gold may be useful. Gold is illustrative of the hard choices we must make as conscious investors and also has a unique role in the history of money. Many speculators have done well with gold as an investment, and a strong contingent of investors prefers gold to the "market." This "noble metal" has, since time immemorial, reminded us of our highest human attributes, and its history is rich with legend and mythology, as well as dire warnings about its allure.

From conquistadors to pirates, from gold bullion locked away to gold nano-particles used in technology, this metal weighs heavily on our minds. But the mining practices now employed for extracting this rare metal should give us pause. Cyanide is currently used to release small remnants of precious gold from the very impure exploitable deposits. This deadliest of poisons may one day taint the water sources of one-fourth of Chile's land and 6 percent of Argentina's. Enough water to quench the annual thirst of a city is ruined forever each day, and sacred mountains are being processed into rubble—for what? Jewelry? As security against currency devaluations? What are we thinking?

In ancient times, gold was revered as liquid sun and only used in the temples of the mysteries. Thousands of years ago, the Lydians formed gold into coins before their hoard was captured by the Persians. Eventually the depictions of gods, goddesses, lions, bulls, and owls on coins were replaced by the visages of Alexander the Great and the Caesars. In the transactional space of commerce, coins no longer were a reminder of the spirit in matter; instead, they began to reflect and manifest political power.

From 8000 B.C. up to the Renaissance, a remnant of the mystical attitude toward gold lived on in the mysteries of South America. The Incas put no monetary value on this substance and generously used it to line their holy stone temples. Legend describes a great golden disc that was seen as a doorway to the sun in the temple in Cusco. This may have been the only gold saved from the conquistadors. The Incas apparently safely buried this spiritual portal in the depths of Lake Titicaca; scuba divers have been searching for it for decades.

The Templars, a group of warrior monks prominent during the Crusades, had a special connection to Solomon's temple in Jerusalem and the "golden section," the mysterious ratio behind the temple's design. This formula describes much about the order of the universe and provides humanity with an inner sense of proportion. After returning to France from the Holy Land, when given property to build on, the Templars discovered that they had built their monastery on top of a mother lode of gold. The monks were sworn to poverty, yet, because of these riches, were instrumental in financing roads and universities all over Europe.

In a determined act of greed, the jealous King of France, Philip the Beautiful, made a deal with the Pope to excommunicate the monks, confiscate their wealth, torture them into confessing distorted truths, and burn them at the stake for sacrilege. Interestingly, Pope Benedict XVI only recently, at the end of his tenure, lifted this curse on the Templars almost 700 years later!

Though ancient forms of paper money certainly existed in the East, the Templars set a precedent by providing receipts for pilgrims' gold. These receipts were recognized in Jerusalem, so that the pilgrims would have nothing of apparent value to lose to robbers on the way.

In the 1700s, such receipts were given out by goldsmiths who stored gold for customers until the son of a Scottish goldsmith,

John Law, persuaded the impoverished king of France to do the same: to print and trade the receipts. This convenient exchange led to the formation of one of the first state banks. At that time, the Duke of Orleans fired all the court alchemists who had been desperately employed to figure out how to turn lead into gold. Paper receipts made actual gold less critical to produce, since the receipts could be printed without real gold to back it up.

This was the beginning of derivatives and speculation. The volatile but convenient system gained favor all over Europe and in the New World, especially after the Gold Rush of 1848 that prompted 300,000 prospectors to move to California. In general, the gold-panners made less money than the merchants who took their gold, converted it into paper currency, and stored it in local banks.

The practice of printing money limited to the amount of gold actually owned came to be known as the "gold standard." London adopted a gold standard in 1860 that lasted until 1931, when imports exceeded exports and the gold ran out. Germany had already stopped in 1914—it was simpler just to print money with nothing to back it!

After the Second World War, American currency was still at least partially backed by gold in Fort Knox, and the leaders of the Western World agreed to base the value of each country's currency on the U.S. dollar. This was fine in the booming 1950s, but in the 1960s massive spending on the war in Vietnam depleted our stores of gold.

At a certain point, President De Gaulle of France demanded that the U.S. export some gold to prove we had it. Nixon refused, and in 1971 called for a new "free flowing value system." In other words, money became totally uprooted from gold, and the world's policymakers could print and exchange as much paper money as they wanted. This led to the hyperinflation unfairly attributed to President Carter.

Meanwhile, Nixon had already clinched a deal with OPEC

ABOUT THE AUTHOR

The sad reality is that money has driven war and global dysfunction for over a century. But there now is an urgent sense of possibility that we can turn the tide and invest in peace.

Perhaps this sense of possibility is in my blood. My grandfather, Hiram Bingham III, uncovered the sacred site of Machu Picchu in 1911, opening an important portal between the sacred nature of the southern Andes and the rest of the world. I see my professional life as an adventure in the cement jungles of the financial world. My goal is for money to be used as a sacred tool and common ritual for connecting cultures, peoples, and businesses globally.

This spiritual view of money was nurtured through discussions with my father, Hiram IV, a retired diplomat with a missionary zeal for the teachings of the Austrian philosopher Rudolf Steiner. "Harry" Bingham angered the German Vichy government by continuing to issue visas to Jewish families after being told not to do so. My father taught me to live out of my ideals and to "give the best that I have to the best that I know."

Growing up as the tenth child at the tail end of a once-enormous inheritance afforded me a unique window into the world of the wealthy. Our family was accepted into country clubs and private schools on scholarship while needing to live simply and frugally at home. My father especially liked to talk about different ways of thinking about money and economics. He taught me to look at sunsets upside down and backwards through my legs, so that I would see the colors fresh. I remember being astonished to see green in the sunset. Perhaps that was his greatest legacy for me: looking at everything, including money, from a fresh perspective!

• • •

After twelve years managing public and private investment portfolios, G. Benjamin Bingham founded and now operates a sustainable financial management company, along with an accompanying research arm and proprietary fund family. More information can be found www.missionmarkets.com.

Mr. Bingham is a Fellow of Economists for Peace and Security. He is a member of the Investors' Circle and the Social Venture Network, and, as a social entrepreneur/investor/money manager, draws on broad hands-on management experience at two technology startups, one in biological healthcare (Demegen) and the other a global workflow solution provider (Anthurium Solutions).

Mr. Bingham is a Registered Investment Advisor with a CFP designation and a background in philanthropy. He is on the board of the Mariah Fenton Gladis Foundation and CSRHub, the largest data source for ratings of corporations on environmental, social, and governance issues. He attended Groton School, Yale University, and Emerson College in England. He writes regularly for *The Huffington Post*.

SOURCES

[1] "The Global Impact Investor Network." www.thegiin.org/

[2] "Impact Investing Policy Collaborative (IIPC)." http://iipcollaborative.org/

[3] *The Impact Investor* project—a research collaboration between Insight at Pacific Community Ventures, CASE at Duke University, and ImpactAssets—was made possible with the generous support of Omidyar Network, Annie E. Casey Foundation, RS Group, Heron Foundation, W. K. Kellogg Foundation, and Deutsche Bank. This article is an edited excerpt from the final project report published in November 2013, *Impact Investing 2.0: The Way Forward—Insight from 12 Outstanding Funds*. The twelve firms and funds studied include Aaavishkaar, Accion Texas, Bridges Ventures, Business Partners Limited, Calvert Foundation, Deutsche Bank, Elevar, Huntington Capital, The W. K. Kellogg Foundation, MicroVest, RSF Social Finance, and SEAF.

[4] Detailed case studies, information on our research methods, and full findings are available at the Impact Investing 2.0 project microsite: www.pacificcommunityventures.org/impinv2.

[5] Casey, Tina. "Sahara Forest Project Grows Green Jobs From Sand, Saltwater, & CO2." *CleanTechnica* (13 Jan 2013). http://cleantechnica.com/2013/01/29/sahara-forest-project-grows-green-jobs-in-desert/

[6] Overton, Thomas. "World's Largest Fuel Cell Plant Opens in South Korea." *Power Magazine* (25 Feb 2014). www.powermag.com/worlds-largest-fuel-cell-plant-opens-in-south-korea/

[7] de Paula, Matthew. "Audi Says Synthetic 'E-Fuel' From Microorganisms Is Better Than Gas Or Diesel." *Forbes* (1 Jan 2014). www.forbes.com/sites/matthewdepaula/2014/01/31/audi-tests-synthetic-e-fuel-derived-from-microorganisms/

[8] McMahon, Jeff. "NASA: A Nuclear Reactor To Replace Your Water Heater." *Forbes* (22 Feb 2013). www.forbes.com/sites/jeffmcmahon/2013/02/22/nasa-a-nuclear-reactor-to-replace-your-water-heater/

[9] "The Reinvestment Fund." www.trfund.com/

[10] "RSF Social Finance." http://rsfsocialfinance.org/

[11] "Generation." https://www.generationim.com/

[12] Steiner, Rudolf. *Rethinking Economics: Lectures and Seminars on World Economics* (Great Barrington, MA: SteinerBooks) 2013.

[13] Schumacher, E. F. *Small is Beautiful: Economics As If People Mattered* (New York: Harper & Row, 1973).

[14] Kanzer, Adam. "Let's Stop Investing Our Retirement Funds in Lethal Weapons." *Reuters* Blog (9 Jan 2013). http://blogs.reuters.com/great-debate/2013/01/09/lets-stop-investing-our-retirement-funds-in-lethal-weapons/

[15] "HIP Investor." http://hipinvestor.com/about-us/

[16] Marcum, David, and Stephen Smith. *Egonomics: What Makes Ego Our Greatest Asset (Or Most Expensive Liability)* (New York: Simon & Schuster) 2007.

[17] "S&P 500 Return Calculator." http://dqydj.net/sp-500-return-calculator/

[18] "U.S. Inflation Calculator" www.usinflationcalculator.com/

[19] "Julia Butterfly Hill: We Live In An Age Of 'Disposability Consciousness.'" *The Huffington Post* (9 July 2010). www.huffingtonpost.com/2010/07/09/understanding-disposabili_n_641070.html

[20] Gage, Deborah. "The Venture Capital Secret: 3 Out of 4 Start-Ups Fail." *The Wall Street Journal* (20 Sept 2012).

[21] Stone, W. Clement. *The Success System That Never Fails* (Englewood Cliffs, NJ: Prentice-Hall) 1962.

[22] Eiseley, Loren. *The Immense Journey* (New York: Random House) 1957.

[23] White, Heather. "Bangladesh - Savar Solutions and Fast Fashion may not be Compatible." *Harvard University Ethics Blog* (16 May

2013) http://ethics.harvard.edu/lab/blog/310-bangladesh-savar-solutions-and-fast-fashion-may-not-be-compatible

[24] Prive, Tanya. "Inside The JOBS Act: Equity Crowdfunding." *Forbes* (6 Nov 2012). www.forbes.com/sites/tanyaprive/2012/11/06/inside-the-jobs-act-equity-crowdfunding-2/

[25] "CSRHub." www.csrhub.com/

[26] "WikiPositive." www.wikipositive.org/

[27] Investors' Circle. www.investorscircle.net/

[28] "Toniic: The Action Community for Global Impact Investing." www.toniic.com/

[29] "Maximpact: Impact Investing Network." www.maximpact.com/

[30] "Mission Markets: The Market for Impact and Sustainable Investing." www.missionmarkets.com/

[31] "Kiva: Loans That Change Lives." www.kiva.org/

[32] "BALLE: Be a Localist." https://bealocalist.org/

[33] "Slow Money. " https://slowmoney.org/

[34] "What Is CSA?" www.justfood.org/csa

[35] Hyde, Lewis. *The Gift: Creativity and the Artist in the Modern World.* (New York: Vintage Books) 2007.

[36] "Solutions for Progress." www.solutionsforprogress.com/

[37] "Anthurium: Changing the Way People Work." www.anthuriumsi.com

[38] Zenger, Jack, and Joseph Folkman. "Are Women Better Leaders Than Men?" *Harvard Business Review* (15 March 2012). https://hbr.org/2012/03/a-study-in-leadership-women-do

[39] "Benjamin Franklin's Intellectual Revolution." *NPR* (5 July 2013). www.npr.org/2013/07/05/199025503/benjamin-franklins-intellectual-revolution

[40] "Fundrise: The Real Estate Crowdfunding Marketplace." https://fundrise.com/

[41] "Cutting Edge Capital: Capital Raising and Ownership Structure." www.cuttingedgecapital.com/

[42] "Indiegogo: Global Crowdfunding Engine to Fundraise Online." www.indiegogo.com/

[43] "AEO: Association for Enterprise Opportunity." www.micro enterpriseworks.org/

[44] "AEO: Association for Enterprise Opportunity." *To Catch a Dollar.* www.tocatchadollar.com/partners/association-for-enterprise-opportunity/

[45] "Opportunity Collaboration." www.opportunitycollaboration.net

[46] "MicroCredit Enterprises." www.mcenterprises.org/

[47] Bank, David. "E+Co Avoids Liquidation, Barely, and Emerges Persistent." *The Huffington Post* (3 Oct 2012). www.huffington post.com/david-bank/eco-avoids-liquidation-ba_b_1932503.html

[48] "Ethical Markets." www.ethicalmarkets.com/

[49] "About Us." http://hipinvestor.com/about-us/

[50] "The Four System Conditions of a Sustainable Society." *The Natural Step.* www.naturalstep.org/the-system-conditions

[51] "The Natural Step." www.naturalstep.org/

[52] "350." http://350.org/

[53] "Understanding 350." http://archive.350.org/understanding-350

[54] "Jonathan Rose Companies." www.rosecompanies.com

[55] "5 Stone Green Capital 5SGC." www.5sgc.com/

[56] "Amero Global Investors." www.ameroglobalinvestors.com/

[57] Waage, Sissel, and Edward Cameron. "Is It Time to Divest from Fossil Fuels?" *GreenBiz* (2 August 2013). www.greenbiz.com/blog/2013/08/02/thinking-unthinkable-it-time-divest-unburnable-fossil-fuels

[58] Andresen, Tino. "EON Banks on Renewables in Split From Conventional Power." *Bloomberg* (1 Dec 2014). www.bloomberg.com/news/2014-11-30/eon-banks-on-renewables-with-plan-to-spin-off-conventional-power.html

[59] "Resilient Portfolios & Fossil-Free Pensions." 30 September 2013. http://hipinvestor.com/wp-content/uploads/Resilient-Port-

folios-and-Fossil-Free-Pensions-ByHIPinvestor-GoFossilFree-vFi-
nal-2014Jan21.pdf

[60] "About B Lab." http://benefitcorp.net/about-b-lab

[61] "ImpactAssets 50." www.impactassets.org/publications_
insights/impact50

[62] "Endobility." www.endobility.com/

[63] "Trust Across America." www.trustacrossamerica.com/

[64] "About Ashoka's Empathy Initiative." http://empathy.
ashoka.org/about-ashokas-empathy-initiative

[65] "Verité: Fair Labor. Worldwide." www.verite.org/

[66] "SVT Group: Impact Accounting." http://svtgroup.net/

[67] Hawken, Paul. *Blessed Unrest: How the Largest Movement in
the World Came Along, and Why No One Saw It Coming* (New York:
Viking) 2007.

[68] "KINS Innovation Networks." www.kinsinnovation.org/

[69] Foulkes, Imogen. "Swiss to Vote on Incomes for All—
Working or Not." *BBC* (17 Dec 2013).

[70] "Triodos Bank." www.triodos.com/en/about-triodos-bank/

[71] "RSF Social Finance." http://rsfsocialfinance.org/

[72] "Natural Investments, LLC." http://naturalinvesting.com/

[73] "CenterPoint Advisors." http://centerpointadvisors.net/

[74] Urban Investments: Social Impact Bond for Early Childhood Education." *Goldman Sachs.* www.goldmansachs.com/what-
we-do/investing-and-lending/urban-investments/case-studies/salt-l
ake-social-impact-bond.html

[75] "MicroVest." www.microvestfund.com/

[76] "TriLinc Global: Invest with Impact." www.trilincglobal.com/

[77] McDonough, William, and Michael Braungart. *Cradle to
Cradle: Remaking the Way We Make Things* (New York: North Point
Press) 2002.

[78] "EcoTrust Forest Management, Inc." www.ecotrustforests.com/

[79] "The Lyme Timber Company." www.lymetimber.com/

[80] "The Roundtable on Sustainable Palm Oil." www.rspo.org/

[81] "Chinese Workers Pay a Toxic Price for Their Jobs Making

Apple's iPhones and iPads." *PRI* (17 Sept 2014). www.pri.org/stories/2014-09-17/chinese-workers-pay-toxic-price-their-jobs-making-apples-iphones-and-ipads

[82] "Accelerating Appalachia." www.acceleratingappalachia.org/

[83] Potter, Wendell. *Deadly Spin: An Insurance Company Insider Speaks Out* (New York: Bloomsbury Press) 2010.

[84] "Wildfires: A Symptom of Climate Change." *NASA* (24 Sept 2010). www.nasa.gov/topics/earth/features/wildfires_prt.htm

[85] Wernick, Adam. "Scotland Launches the World's Largest Tidal Power Project." *PRI* (3 Sept 2014). www.pri.org/stories/2014-09-03/scotland-launches-worlds-largest-tidal-power-project